N.C. WYETH

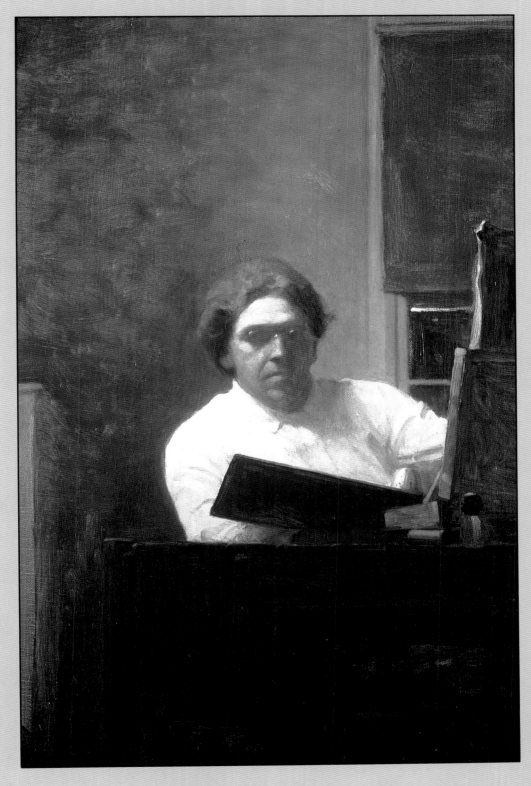

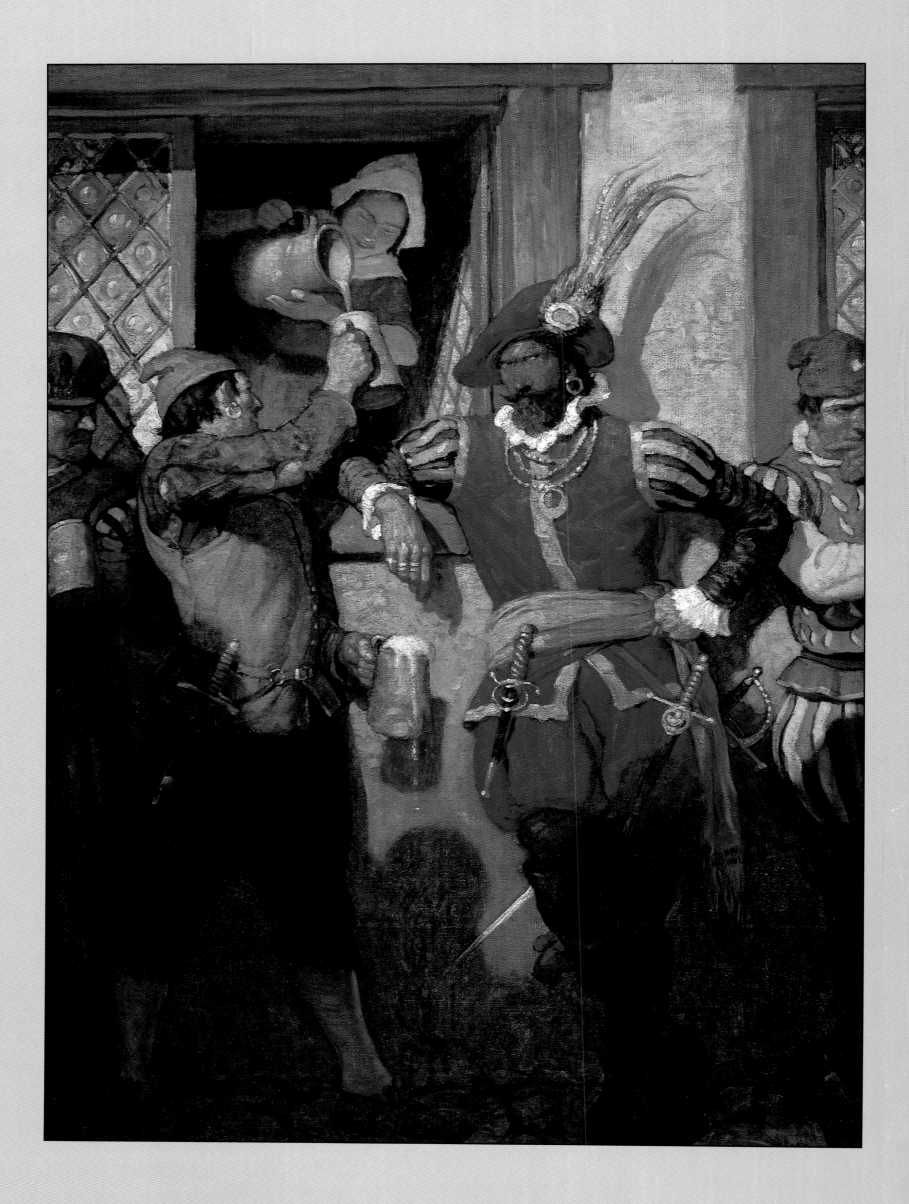

N.C. WYETH

KATE F. JENNINGS

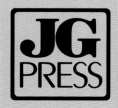

JG PRESS

Page 1: **Self Portrait,** 1913
Oil on canvas, 18¼ × 12¼ in.
Collection of Nicholas Wyeth
Photograph courtesy of the Brandywine River Museum
Photography by Peter Ralston

Page 2: **John Oxenham,** 1920
Westward Ho by Charles Kingsley
Charles Scribner's Sons, 1920
Oil on canvas, 40 × 30 in.
Courtesy of the Brandywine Fantasy Gallery, Chicago, IL

Pages 4-5: **The Chase,** 1916
"The Great West that Was" by Col. William F. Cody
Hearst's Magazine, September 1916
Oil on canvas, 17¼ × 38¼ in.
Collection of First Interstate Bank of Arizona, N.A, Tucson, AZ

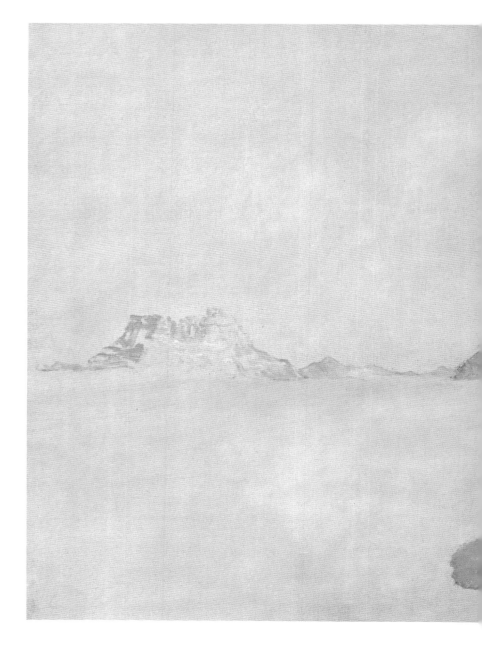

Published by World Publications Group, Inc.
455 Somerset Avenue
North Dighton, MA 02764
www.wrldpub.com

ISBN 1-57215-355-5

Printed and bound in China by Leefung Printers Limited

1 2 3 4 5 06 05 03 02

CONTENTS

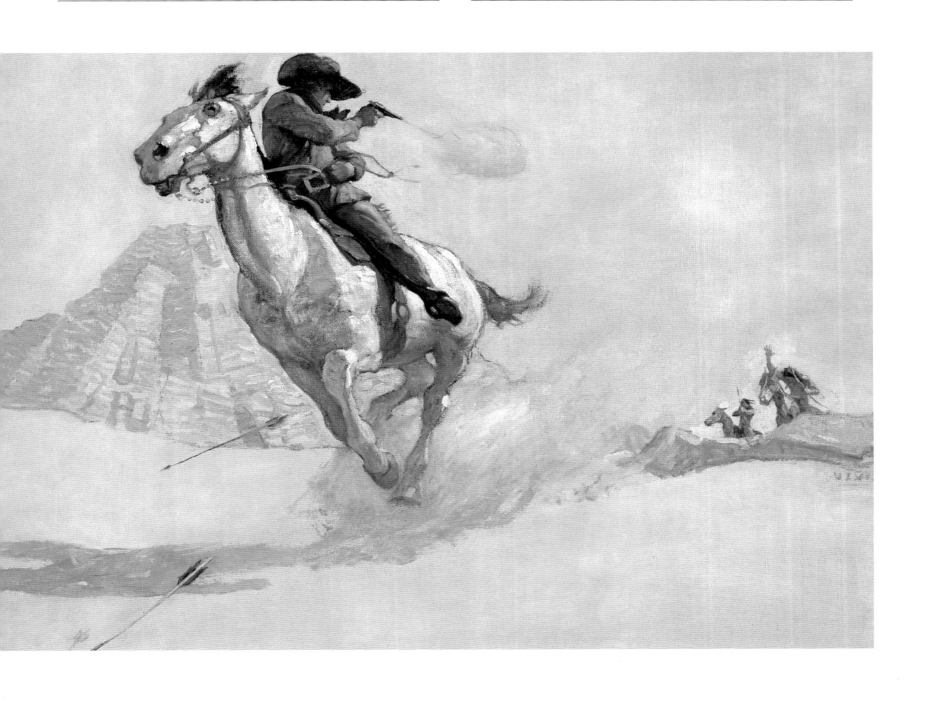

INTRODUCTION

Newell Convers Wyeth, one of America's finest illustrators and the patriarch of an enduring artistic dynasty, was born on October 22, 1882, in the rural township of Needham, Massachusetts.

N.C. Wyeth, called Convers by his family, was the eldest of four sons of Andrew Newell Wyeth II, a farmer of solid New England stock whose ancestors had first landed at Cambridge, Massachusetts, from England in 1645. His mother, Henriette Zirngiebel, was French Swiss. Her father was a horticulturist who at one time was the Director of the Harvard Botanical Gardens.

The chores and activities of a farming household formed the structure of Wyeth's boyhood, instilling in him an abiding respect for nature, the bounty of the land, and a lifelong affection for animals of many species. He enjoyed the strenuous physical labor required to prepare the fields, to plant, and to harvest their crops; these routine tasks gave N.C. Wyeth a deep understanding of the human form in motion. He had a vivid sense of its muscular framework, weight, mass, and the diverse range of gestural expressions. The early years that he spent plowing, scything and baling hay, milking cows, tending the livestock with a team of horses, and confronting the elements were a primary source of subjects in his paintings, posters, and murals.

Wyeth had an extraordinary capacity for recalling exact visual details, moods of weather, seasonal changes in landscapes, and even scents and sounds connected with particular days and events.

At times, his potent reveries would afflict him with melancholy and a yearning for the beauty and simplicity of the past he remembered. Yet their strength seems also to have sustained a prolific and intensely productive career.

To his father's chagrin and consternation, N.C. Wyeth was not an avid student, preferring to spend his free moments

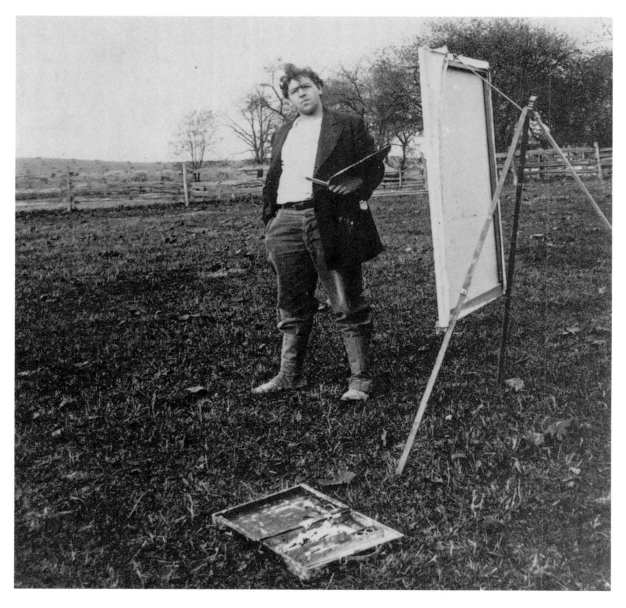

Left: N.C. Wyeth painting on his farm in Chadds Ford, Pennsylvania. Wyeth often used his familiar environs as a backdrop in his work.

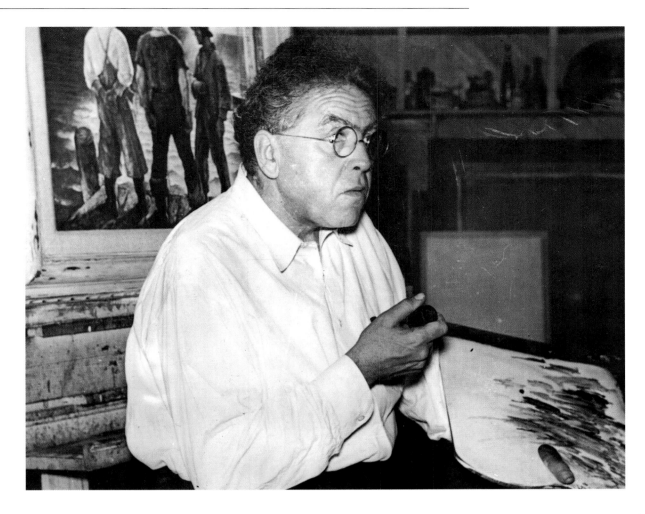

Right: Wyeth in his studio with his paintings, *Three Fishermen*, c. 1938, in the background.

sketching. Fortunately for Convers, his mother encouraged his predilection for drawing. She interceded on his behalf when his father wanted to send him to New Hampshire to be a farmer's apprentice at age sixteen. Instead, she persuaded her husband to allow Convers to attend the Mechanic Arts School in Boston, where he learned drafting and graduated in 1899. More intent on an artistic profession than with drafting, Convers persuaded his father to send him to the Massachusetts Normal Arts School. Here his potential for illustration was recognized by a teacher, Richard Andrew, who suggested Convers continue with his studies at the Eric Pape School of Art in Boston, which he did during the winter and spring of 1902.

Following this, Convers continued his studies with a book illustrator, Charles Reed. When a friend and fellow artist, Clifford Ashley, returned home from Wilmington, Delaware, in the summer of 1902, he encouraged N.C. Wyeth to join him at the Howard Pyle School there. Tuition was free but students were accepted on a trial basis; hard work and artistic ability were essential for full acceptance. Wyeth arrived in Wilmington on his twentieth birthday and within four months was a full-fledged associate.

His first sale of his work was to the *Saturday Evening Post* for a painting of a bucking bronco and cowboy. It appeared on their cover on February 21, 1903. For this illustration the *Saturday Evening Post* paid fifty dollars. A month later *Success* magazine used Wyeth's canvas of two railroad surveyors perched precariously atop a mountain ravine. *Success* paid thirty dollars for this work, which appeared in the March 1903 issue. The dramatic tension of the pose and central focus of the image's pictorial elements were keynotes of Wyeth's style.

N.C. Wyeth's education and experiences under the tutelage of Howard Pyle was a fertile and productive period of his life. His technical progress seemed to increase exponentially each month with corollary requests from publishers and periodicals. In Wilmington, he rented a room on Adams Street for two dollars a week and a studio for four dollars a month. He was able to hire a model for twenty cents an hour.

In the summertime the school moved to the neighboring countryside of Chadds Ford, Pennsylvania, where classes were held within the lofts of a vacant grist mill. This spacious and romantic setting was ideal for encouraging the young artists. In an article in the *Christian Science Monitor* on November 13, 1912, Wyeth described his mentor in a passage that displays the artist's narrative gifts:

> My most vivid recollection of Howard Pyle was gained during the first five minutes I knew him. He stood with his back to the blazing and crackling logs in his studio fireplace, his legs spaced apart, his arms akimbo. His towering figure seemed to lift to greater heights with the swiftly ascending smoke and sparks from the hearth behind him.

Pyle had taught classes at the Drexel Institute in Philadelphia and was a successful and popular illustrator. He was a frequent contributor to *Harper's Monthly* and *Century* magazines and produced book illustrations for Houghton Mifflin, among other publishers.

Howard Pyle tempered and distilled the forceful enthusiasms of his pupil, honing his technique to suit not only the requirements of magazine illustration, but also to elucidate

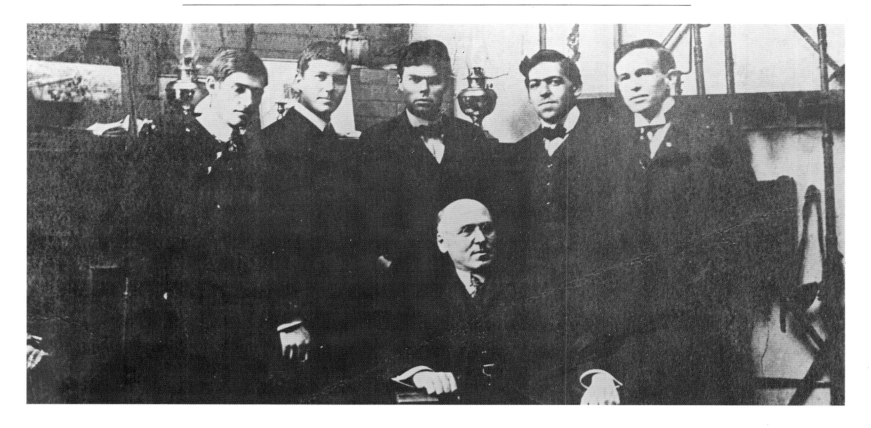

Above: Howard Pyle (seated) and his students (left to right) Clifford Ashley, Gordon McCouch, Thornton Oakley, N.C. Wyeth, and Allan True, c. 1903.

Below: Wyeth's *Sketch of a Man on a Bucking Bronco,* painted in 1902.

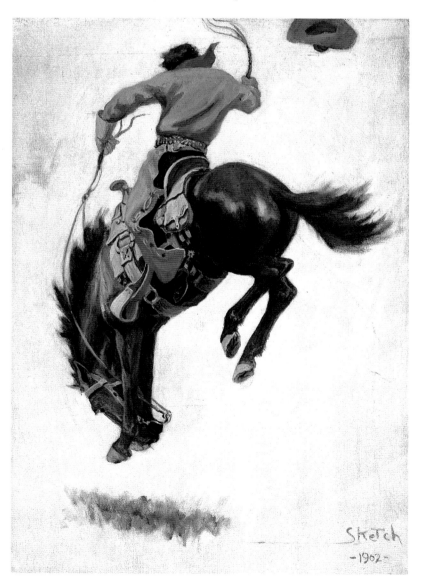

certain painterly standards and to satisfy the artist's personal intentions. Wyeth wrote:

> Mr. Pyle's inordinate ability as a teacher lay primarily in his sense of penetration; to read beneath the crude lines on paper the true purpose, to detect therein our real inclinations and impulses. Wretched, unstable drawing would quickly assume coherent shape and character; raw and uncouth conceptions would become softened and refined, until in a marvelously short time the student would find himself and converge upon that elevation of thinking and feeling which would disclose before him a limitless horizon of possibilities.

The group of artists was close-knit, ambitious, and talented and their work was readily in demand in New York. During one month in the fall of 1905, Pyle and his students were represented in such magazines as *Outing, Metropolitan, Scribner's,* and *Harper's.*

Pyle did not limit his program of instruction to repetitive classroom study. When a fire swept the city of Baltimore in February of 1904, he quickly contacted *Collier's Magazine* and arranged a paid assignment for his protegés whose sketches would report on the event as it unfolded. They boarded a train posthaste to the scene. Here Wyeth learned the value of first-hand experience to convey a sense of immediacy, drama, and compassion in his illustrations and paintings. Wyeth wrote to his mother of the destruction he witnessed:

> The sights I saw from now on I cannot describe – everything aglow – immense high walls balancing and swaying like sheets of paper in the stiff wind, which was continually sweeping over the place, whistling and moaning through these Pompeian towers, huge pieces of tin flapping and banging on the tops of these towers like the wings of some colossal bat, while all around us were explosions and bursts of green flames darting out from under tremendously

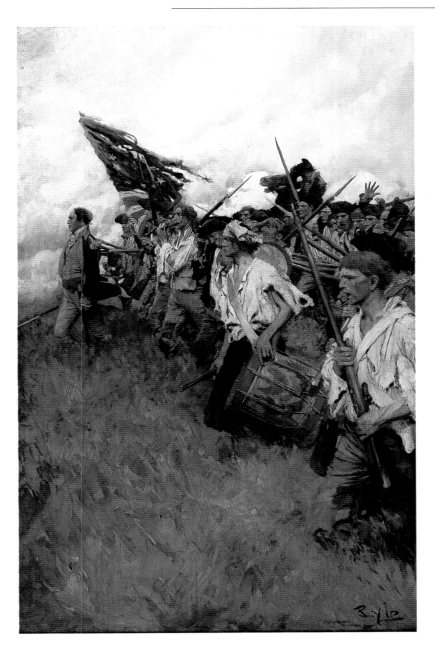

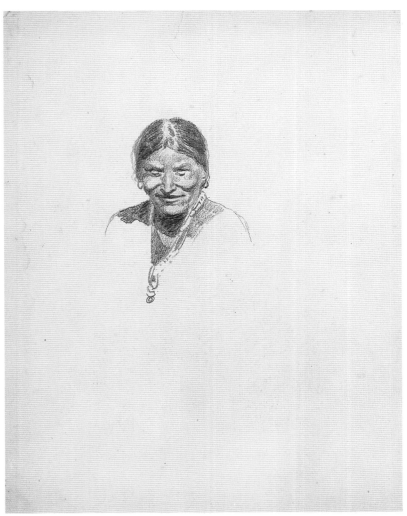

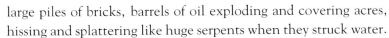

Left: Howard Pyle's *The Nationmakers*, painted in 1903.

Above: A pencil sketch by Wyeth, *Head of an Indian Woman*, done in 1904.

large piles of bricks, barrels of oil exploding and covering acres, hissing and splattering like huge serpents when they struck water.

In May of 1904, Charles Scribner and Sons gave N.C. Wyeth his first book to illustrate, *Boys of St. Timothy's* by Arthur Stanwood Pier, and the course of his career was shaped by the success of this project. On his visits to New York, Wyeth took advantage of the opportunity to visit art galleries and museums and he was particularly impressed by the canvases of Frederic Remington.

After graduating from the Howard Pyle School, he planned an excursion out West sponsored by the *Saturday Evening Post* and *Scribner's Magazine,* who were interested in a documentary story complete with drawings and full-color canvases of his expedition and the characters he encountered.

On September 24, 1904, N.C. Wyeth embarked on the tedious, fifty-four-hour train ride to Denver, traveling through the desolate flatlands and monotonous farm country of the Midwest. In Denver he stayed with the family of a fellow student from Wilmington, Alan True. In addition to their hospitality, the Trues gave Convers permits to visit local Indian reservations. He purchased the requisite gear for his ranching sojourn including a saddle, bridle, chaps, rain slicker, boots,

spurs, britches, and blankets – all for approximately fifty-five dollars – and then hopped a train for Deer Trail, Colorado.

This was a ramshackle town with only a saloon, dry goods store, train station, and post office, and here Wyeth met up with a sheepherder who would take him farther along. After a series of unexpected events, including an antelope hunt and the rescue of a ranch wagon stuck on a trail, Wyeth reached his destination – Elroy Gill's ranch. The first narrative tale of Wyeth's adventures was "A Day with the Round-Up" published in March 1906. His concise declarative sentences suit the taciturn nature of the cowboys and cattle ranchers who were his companions, and they match the spare, austere beauty of the desert and Rocky Mountains.

The cowpunchers would gather about 125 horses, then rope out one with the right brand from their ranch to ride that morning. Wyeth spent one day herding 300 head of cattle through Rattlesnake Gulch and though the conditions were often rough, dangerous, and physically demanding, and the hours long, the artist thrived.

Wyeth saw a young boy killed when a horse kicked his head at a broncobusting contest and he watched a black man throw a wild steer to the ground by sinking his teeth into its nose and tossing it. Hunting antelope and shooting prairie dogs for target

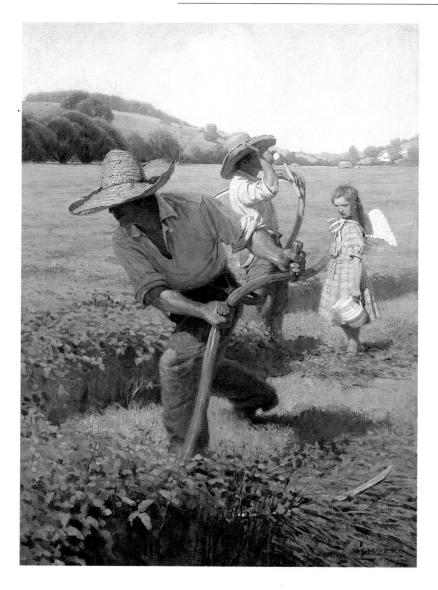

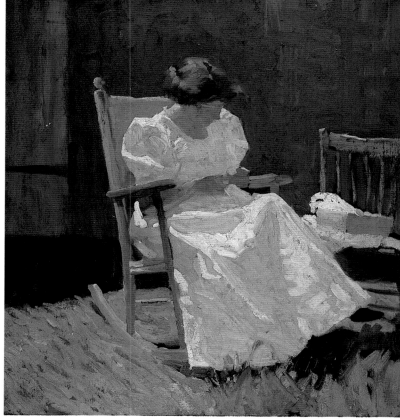

Left: Wyeth's *The Scythers*, painted in 1908.

Above: *Mrs. N.C. Wyeth in Rocking Chair*, completed c. 1916.

Opposite: Wyeth in costume as Little John.

practice were typical pastimes of the hired hands. Wyeth conducted a fair bit of trading and bargaining to accumulate a collection of costumes and artifacts for his illustrations. Any spare moments were used for sketching the cowpunchers, the broncos, and the vast, mountainous expanse.

After a month or so, Convers struck out for Durango, Colorado, from where he took a stagecoach to Muddy Springs, Arizona. Here he lost his hard-earned cash, amounting to between $350 to $400, when a band of Mexicans raided a government post. He got a job as a mail carrier between Muddy Springs and Fort Defiance, Arizona, riding the eighty-five mile distance every three days or so. It was a bitterly cold and exhausting trek during November and December, setting out alone through snow drifts and windstorms, but in one month he saved enough for his passage back East. He was eager to return to the familiar landscape of Wilmington and its environs, and to his cherished friends.

Convers spent New Year's Eve of 1904 with Carolyn Bockius, who was soon to become his fiancé, and he felt unusually positive about his prospects for the future. When he wrote to his mother of his engagement he began the letter, "The skies are brightening, the light glow of success is gradually throwing its soft light on my path. May it continue."

In March 1905, Wyeth went to Theodore Roosevelt's inauguration in Washington, D.C., accompanied by another artist, Harvey Dunn. By dressing in western-style outfits, they were able to join a group of cowboys; they told the cowboys they had traveled from New Mexico and South Dakota. Instead of merely watching from the sidewalk, they were given two mounts to ride along with the inaugural parade.

Wyeth continued with his western illustrations, portraying Kit Carson and Cree Indians in pictures for the *Saturday Evening Post* and Eskimos for *Harper's Monthly*. In his leisure time, he went canoeing with Miss Bockius on the Delaware River. While she ventured north to meet his parents, he and his three brothers, Ed, Nat, and Stimson, took one of their annual walking trips in the hills of Vermont. The strong bonds among the Wyeth sons were reaffirmed on these yearly retreats when they hunted, fished, and camped out in northern New England. Convers reveled in the peaceful, simple beauty of these natural settings as had his favorite author, Henry David Thoreau.

In late February 1906, N.C. Wyeth returned to the West, this time on behalf of *Outing Magazine*, which required illustrations for a story on mining engineering. He took a job stoking the fires on a work train, traveled to railroad construction camps, and picked up all kinds of Indian curios at local stops. These included squaw dresses, a beaded vest, a silver belt, tom-toms, buckskin leggings, and a Mexican sombrero – costumes to be saved for models back home.

After his return he made preparations for his wedding to Carolyn Bockius, whom he married on April 16, 1906, and the furnishing of their first house, a rental in Wilmington. He painted a variety of Indian canvases that were published as prints and offered in a series called "Solitude" to readers of *Outing*.

Wyeth grew distant from Howard Pyle, in part because of his former teacher's demands on his time and creative expression. Pyle had taken a position as an art editor and tried to bolster his own magazine assignments with assurances of additional work by Convers. Wyeth resented the pressure Pyle exerted and resisted his offers whenever possible. Like many talented artists, the student would soon surpass his master in the quality, quantity, and diversity of his paintings and illustrations.

As early as 1907, Wyeth had begun to feel frustrated with the artistic limitations of his magazine work and for years to come he would chafe under the yoke of these commissions. He yearned to paint the countryside and independent, selective subjects that did not require the props, melodrama, and contrived pictorial relationships necessary to suit commercial ends.

Fortunately, *Scribner's Magazine* presented more congenial work to him at this time in the form of a poem, "Back to the Farm" by Martha Bianchi. His paintings to accompany these stanzas were of farmers and their children in the fields – scything, mowing, and plowing with teams of horses – activities he could observe firsthand in the Chadds Ford region. He could also identify these figures with his own childhood, which lends their gestures and expressions a special poignancy.

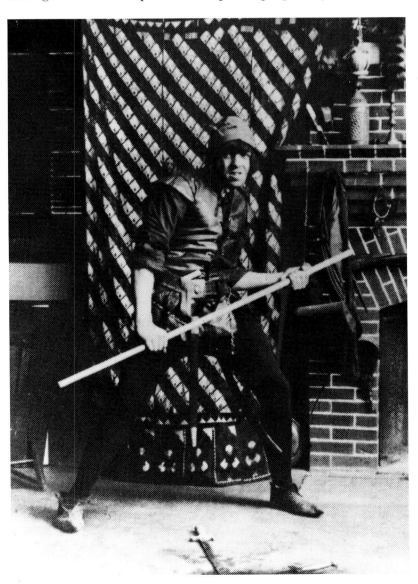

N.C. and Carolyn Wyeth rented a 45-acre farm in Chadds Ford in the fall of 1907. On October 22, 1907, their first daughter Henriette was born on her father's twenty-fifty birthday. Convers cherished the time he was able to spend with her, noting her alertness, intelligence, and humorous deeds in letters to her grandparents.

Wyeth savored the pleasures of rural life and was entertained by visits from his younger brothers and various relatives. He often used his brothers as models, costumed as cowboys and Indians. This may account for the close resemblance many of the figures in his paintings bear to the artist. When possible, he set time aside from his commercial exploits to investigate elements of the surrounding landscape. He felt these sketches were less successful and facile than his other work but they were far more important to him and were distinctly his own. These forays deepened his understanding of technique, color, and living forms.

Wyeth had a low opinion of artists who felt compelled to travel to Europe in search of more interesting themes and continental flourishes. He thought their goals were superficial and that they were abandoning opportunities and fertile topics nearby for the allure of insignificant polish, gloss and glamor. The artists and writers he most admired and respected were impressed by content rather than stylistic flourishes. One of these was Winslow Homer. Wyeth wrote:

> I have come to realize that artistic expression only exists as a serious and valuable possession insofar as one makes it his own. We have such a remarkable example in Homer. He knew light and shade, values, drawing, etc. in common with others. Further than that, *all* he possessed was distinctly his.

Wyeth saw the German Contemporary Exhibition in early 1909 in New York and although the examples he saw did not especially please him, he felt this exposure to different techniques was informative and interesting. Wyeth's second western story "A Sheepherder of the Southwest" appeared in *Scribner's* January 1909 issue. Wyeth chronicled the arduous, solitary existence of a Mexican shepherd that revealed Wyeth's awe for his fortitude and for the spectacular mountain and desert settings.

A second daughter, Carolyn, was born on October 26, 1909, and the event filled him with pride and deepened his love for his own mother. On his twenty-seventh birthday he wrote to her: "I live in hope, Mama, that someday your courage, displayed twenty-seven years ago today and your faithfulness will be rewarded – I shall do my best."

In addition to plentiful requests for western and Indian pictures, in 1910, Wyeth was also entrusted with his first story by Arthur Conan Doyle, a saga of sailing warriors. His complete immersion in this tale is reflected by this letter home:

> Therefore, today, following the seven hours spent with the Saxons, Britons, Huns, Romans; shields, sea axes, spears, cudgels;

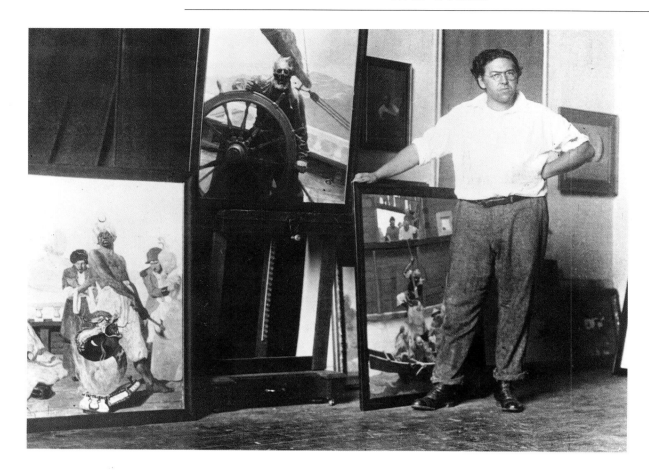

helmets, plumes, fibulae; galleys, keels and lateen sails, my mind sees little more than a kaleidoscopic pageantry of the above – all confusion! However, I am beginning to feel on speaking terms with those hairy Saxons, and when I walk up stairs my legs bend stiff with bronze kneecaps and shin guards, and I duck my head in the doorways lest I knock my shining helmet to the floor.

In the summer of 1910, Wyeth traveled to the fashionable resort in Warm Springs, Virginia, to research families and vistas of the Southern Confederacy for Mary Johnston's book about the Civil War called *The Long Roll.* He was profoundly affected by the sadness and the tragic consequences the war inflicted on the local citizens and their homeland.

In his paintings he was determined to emphasize the suffering these people endured rather than the glories and superficial splendor of war. He also went to the Corcoran Gallery in Washington, D.C. to see a portrait of Stonewall Jackson so that his own illustrations would be accurately detailed. He wrote to Miss Johnston requesting additional guidance:

> I am about the paint the fourth and last picture for the first volume, *The Long Roll* – "The Lovers." The meeting of Colonel Cleave and Judith Cary. . . . What would be her dress? And what sort of outside wrap and bonnet would she wear this spring afternoon if any? And please say a few words about her hair and face. And Colonel Cleave – would he wear a cavalryman's jacket or a coat with skirts? A sash? A soft hat with braid? I find that the selection of his costume is so much a matter of choice. I think it better for you to decide.

The year of 1911 was an unusually eventful and prosperous one for N.C. Wyeth. In March he accepted Scribner's offer to illustrate Robert Louis Stevenson's classic book *Treasure Island.*

In a note to a friend he exclaimed: "The gods have smiled upon me!" With the proceeds from the contract he was able to purchase his own 18-acre farm in Chadds Ford for $2,000 and put down $3,600 as a half-payment for the construction of his house and studio. Wyeth's enthusiasm for his Chester County environs continued: "I'm totally satisfied that this is the little corner of the world wherein I shall work out my destiny. Later on, if the success of my work justifies it, I shall look forward to a summer cottage in New England – but here, I must acknowledge my soul comes nearer to the surface than any other place I know." They would call their homestead "Wyndtryst."

In March 1911, N.C. Wyeth received his first mural commission to produce a series of four life-size Indian pictures for the dining room of the Hotel Utica in Utica, New York. He was especially pleased with this assignment since the hotel's developer, Delos Johnson, had used Frederic Remington and Maxfield Parrish, artists Wyeth respected, for other projects.

In addition to the *Treasure Island* illustrations and Hotel Utica canvases, Wyeth completed an illustrated story for *Scribner's Magazine,* a *Century Magazine* story, a painting for the Forbes Company, and one privately commissioned by a Connecticut sportsman. He thrived on the pressure. "It's no use talking; it's great to be rushed once in a while. Once I get up an impetus, I can work with both hands, painting a blood-curdling pirate fight with one, and with the other, an infant sucking its mother's breast!" In the summertime he and Carolyn took the children to Beach Haven on the New Jersey shore for a respite from the heat and the demands of his commercial work.

On October 24, 1911, Wyeth's first son, Nathaniel Convers Wyeth, was born. Wyeth was always a proud father, buoyed and inspired by the companionship of his children. The only

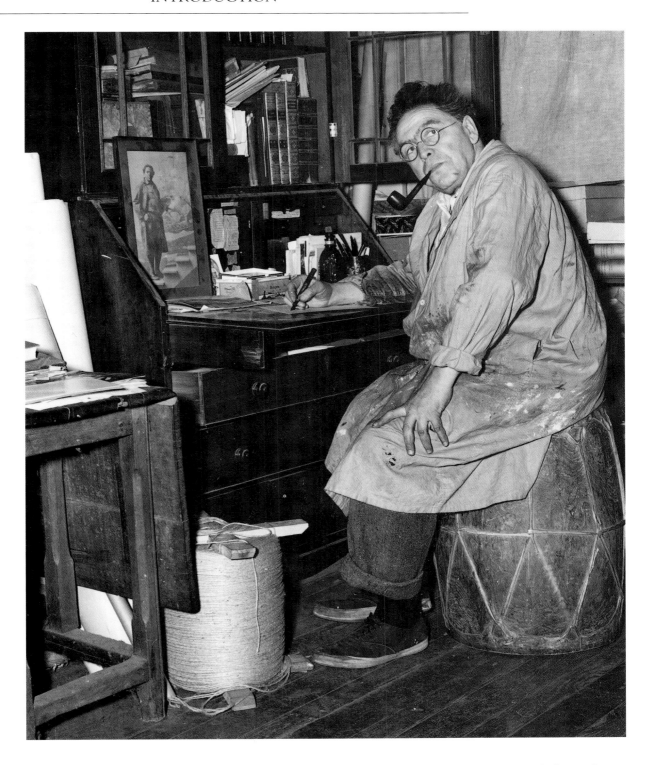

Right: N.C. Wyeth seated on a drum at his desk.

sad note of this busy year was the death of his mentor, Howard Pyle on November 14. Although he had been estranged from his teacher in Pyle's later years, Wyeth was deeply affected by his death and felt an enormous debt to the artist and the man.

> He is gone, there is nothing more to say – all concern now rests with us who came under his masterly influence, to carry on the honest impulses he awakened within us – to perpetuate his *beginning!* . . . I am simply an instrument, fated to have learned from him the first steps and left to approach as near as possible the *unattainable* in art.

Treasure Island was a popular success for Scribner's. Wyeth was highly regarded for his unique facility for creating riveting narrative illustrations in an expedient manner for their classic books and stories. He followed *Treasure Island* with the book *Pike Country Ballads*, magazine illustrations for Civil War stories, *The Story of Christ*, and a series of Finnish legends.

In 1913, Scribner's offered him a second novel by Robert Louis Stevenson, *Kidnapped*, and when he wrote to congratulate his younger brother Stimson on his graduation from Harvard, the letter was filled with parallels to the book's hero David Balfour. "I can see your experience with the covetous old guide on the Island of Mull and the following encounter with the blind beggar with the brace of pistols in his pockets. Then you are a witness to the murder of Roy Campbell of Glenure, the subsequent flight in the heather and your varied life with Alan Breck." Convers's uncanny ability to identify with his characters and his willingness to become absorbed with their exploits lent his paintings their emotional force and perception, in addition to the technical finesse they displayed.

Though he occasionally voiced regret that he lacked the time to enhance his painterly skills, a visit to a show at the Philadelphia Academy of Art in 1914 made him realize and value his artistic gifts:

The occasion has helped me to understand . . . how fortunate I am to be able to illustrate; . . . to have a practical streak, that I can go through life, giving necessary comfort to those dependent upon me and to develop myself under normal conditions, which, made proper use of, should give me health and longevity. . . .

After World War I broke out in Europe, Wyeth was offered a substantial sum by several magazines to join their correspondents and illustrate significant events as they unfolded, but he declined all offers. Wyeth did contribute to the war effort by painting a large mural of Neptune to be used as a poster for the Department of the Navy. He also painted several paintings of the troops for the *Red Cross Magazine* and sent work to exhibitions in St. Louis and to the Panama Pacific Exposition. In 1918 he furnished a 92-foot canvas of American soldiers called *Over the Top.* He was offered the rank of first lieutenant for his work but refused it. This mural was for the New York Treasury Building.

Wyeth's primary concerns during the wartime era were his continuing series of book illustrations, a variety of private commissions, and the care and nurturing of his growing family. His third daughter, Ann, was born on March 15, 1915, and his second son, Andrew, was born on July 12, 1917, the 100th anniversary of Henry David Thoreau's birth. This was a source of joy for Convers, who wrote in 1911 of a biography about Thoreau: "The subtle and glorious glimpse into the life and soul of Thoreau is marvelous and means exceedingly more to me than the Bible and the works of all other men, dead and alive, put together! I believe Thoreau to be the prophet of the future."

Among the novels Wyeth illustrated at this time were Mark Twain's *The Mysterious Stranger,* Robert Louis Stevenson's *Black Arrow,* the autobiography of Buffalo Bill Cody, *Robin Hood* by Paul Creswick, *The Boy's King Arthur* edited by Sidney Lanier, and *The Mysterious Island* by Jules Verne. In 1915 he painted a mural with a marine theme of mermaids and sea dragons for the underground café at the Hotel Traymore in Atlantic City, New Jersey. The hotel was demolished in the 1950s and unfortunately, it is unknown whether the mural was removed and saved.

Even with his prodigious output of canvases, drawings, and decorations, Wyeth was besieged with requests for his work and turned away many assignments. He wrote in April 1916: "There has been so much work offered to me that it has been a constant problem what to take and what to leave."

In 1915, N.C. Wyeth began teaching a small group of four students who met several times a week: once for composition lectures, once on Saturday afternoons for sketch class, and on Sunday evenings for Thoreau readings. One senses that Wyeth felt it was equally important to communicate the philosophical underpinning for his work as well as his technical and mechanical strategies.

He was also continuing the tradition of Howard Pyle, focusing on emotional content, individuality, and meaningful values in his students' work rather than proficiency with picaresque detail and superficial style. Wyeth explained: "All creative expression, be it in painting, writing, or music, if it pretends to appeal warmly and eloquently, must spring from the artist's own factual and emotional experience." He recommended to a friend: Keep your details true but subordinate.

Wyeth's prolific production of illustrations continued after the war and into the 1920s, with increasing requests for public murals, memorials, and decorative panels. In 1918 a New York advertising agency tried to lure Wyeth into an exclusive contract for $20,000 per year that would have required only a limited number of assignments, but he bridled at the suggestion of restricting his creative opportunities. Instead, he directed his energies and enthusiasm to a variety of historical canvases and heroic tales.

Wyeth traveled to the Adirondack Mountains to research his canvases for *The Last of the Mohicans.* For these wilderness

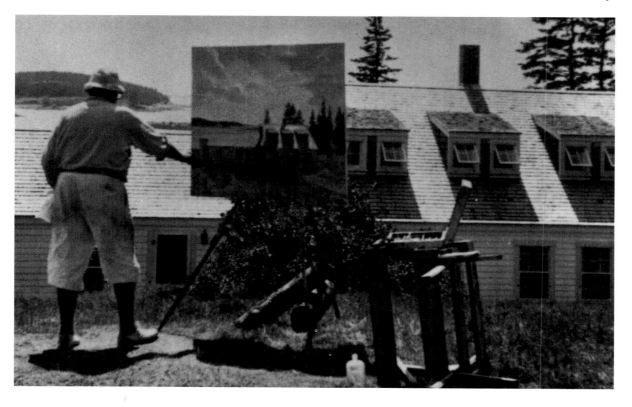

Left: Wyeth painting outside the Wyeth summer home in Port Clyde, Maine, in 1936.

Opposite: The Wyeths in 1922. Seated (left to right): Ann, Mrs. Wyeth, Andy, and Nat; standing (left to right): Carolyn, N.C., and Henriette.

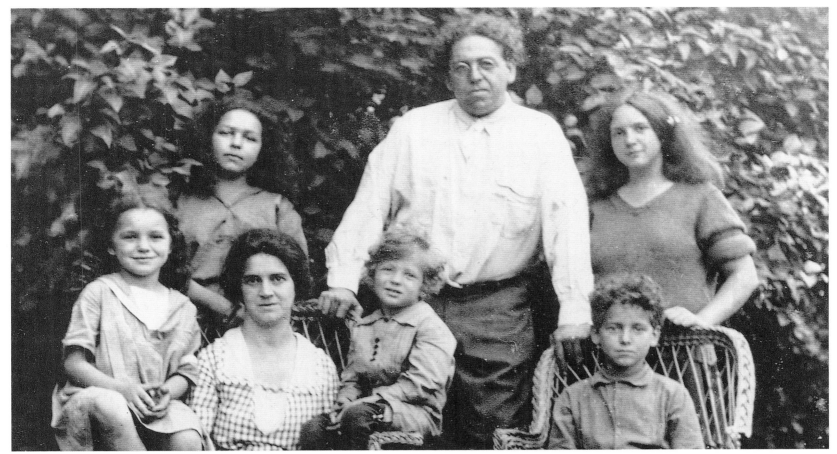

and Indian paintings, he called upon his own canoeing experiences on the Charles and Delaware rivers. He was also at work on canvases for *The Courtship of Miles Standish*, *Robinson Crusoe*, and *Westward Ho!* By this time Wyeth had financial arrangements with several of his publishers who paid royalties to him as a percentage of the number of books sold.

Wyeth's children were beginning to reveal their own artistic sensibilities, particularly Henriette, his eldest daughter. She studied with her father in his studio and he marveled at her instinctive grasp of the intricacies of perspective. Watching his children doing their sketches one evening in 1920, Convers remarked: "Drawing! – that's the outstanding stunt in this house, and to see the whole five around the lamp at night, each one seriously bent over a tablet of paper, recording all sorts of facts and fictions of Nature, one would guess it were organized night art school – or that all were nutty in the same way!"

In the summer of 1921, Wyeth took his family back to his hometown of Needham, Massachusetts, for a year. He had longed to be closer to his parents, his brothers, and the New England region for several years and to acquaint his children with the community there. Although he would later return to their home in Chadds Ford, he was busy with several Boston murals throughout his stay. For the Federal Reserve Bank in Boston he painted two 10- by 13-foot panels, one of Alexander Hamilton and George Washington, the second of Abraham Lincoln and Salmon Chase.

The Wyeths visited Port Clyde, Maine, during the 1910s to 1920s where Convers good friend Sidney Chase had a home. Although Wyeth bought a sea captain's home there in 1920, which had belonged to a Captain Seavy, extensive renovations were in order on the house and the Wyeths did not spend extended periods of time there until the 1930s. Wyeth named his home there "Eight Bells" after the Winslow Homer painting of sailors off the Maine coast.

The family moved back to Pennsylvania in 1923 and Wyeth began a variety of new and challenging projects. He worked on a series of religious paintings for a book about the parables of Christ. Wyeth was a deeply spiritual man and these canvases express a certain emotional transport and awe that illuminates the biblical text.

Several of N.C. Wyeth's children were developing into successful painters alongside their father. Henriette enrolled in the Pennsylvania Academy of Fine Arts in 1923. Andrew was already revealing a precocious talent in his drawings and canvases and Convers took great pleasure in nurturing his skills.

Convers also enjoyed his daughter Ann's talent as a pianist and promoted its expression with musical evenings at home listening to classical music and with visits to the Philadelphia Orchestra. At age nineteen Ann wrote a composition entitled "Christmas Fantasy" that was performed by the Philadelphia Orchestra, conducted by Leopold Stokowski. Ann later married one of N.C. Wyeth's students, John McCoy, in 1935 and her father was thrilled with this fortuitous event.

Nathaniel Wyeth had always shown an interest in constructing model sailboats, practical objects, and even a special fortress of a castle with turrets for his brother Andrew. Later he would be named the first senior engineering fellow at the Du Pont Company, their highest technical position at the time.

Carolyn Wyeth loved animals even as a young girl, with a special fondness for all the domestic creatures on their farm in Chadds Ford. She too became a painter, and her works are prized for their intense originality and brooding nature.

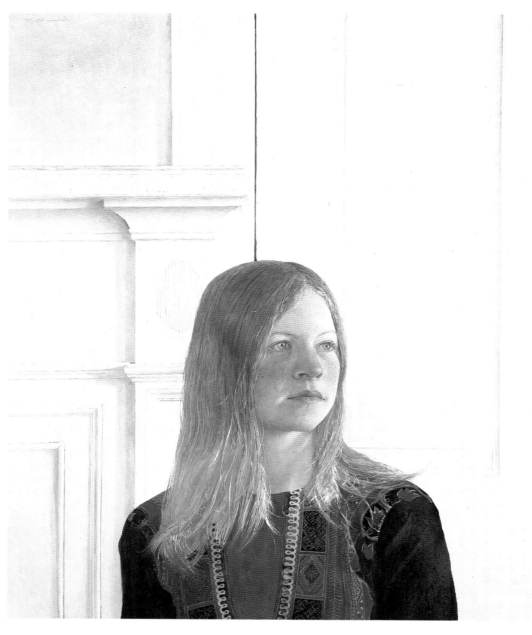

Left: *Siri*, 1970, by N.C. Wyeth's son Andrew.

Below: *Portrait of Pig*, 1970, by Andrew Wyeth's son Jamie.

Right: N.C. Wyeth.

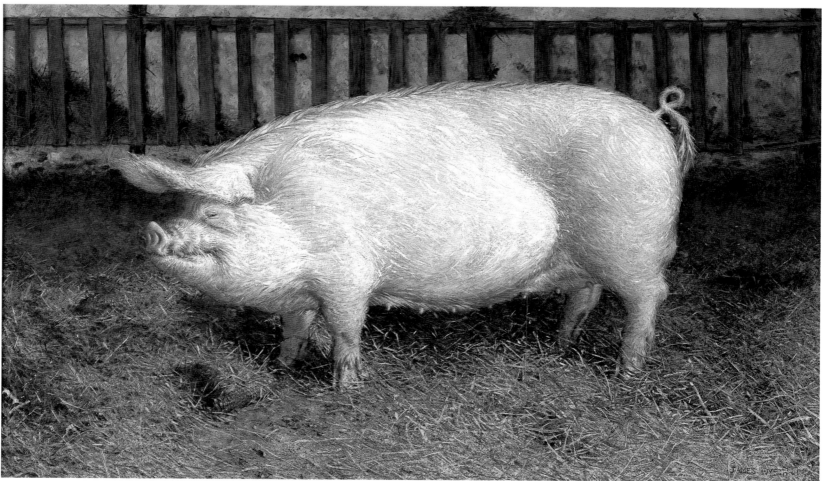

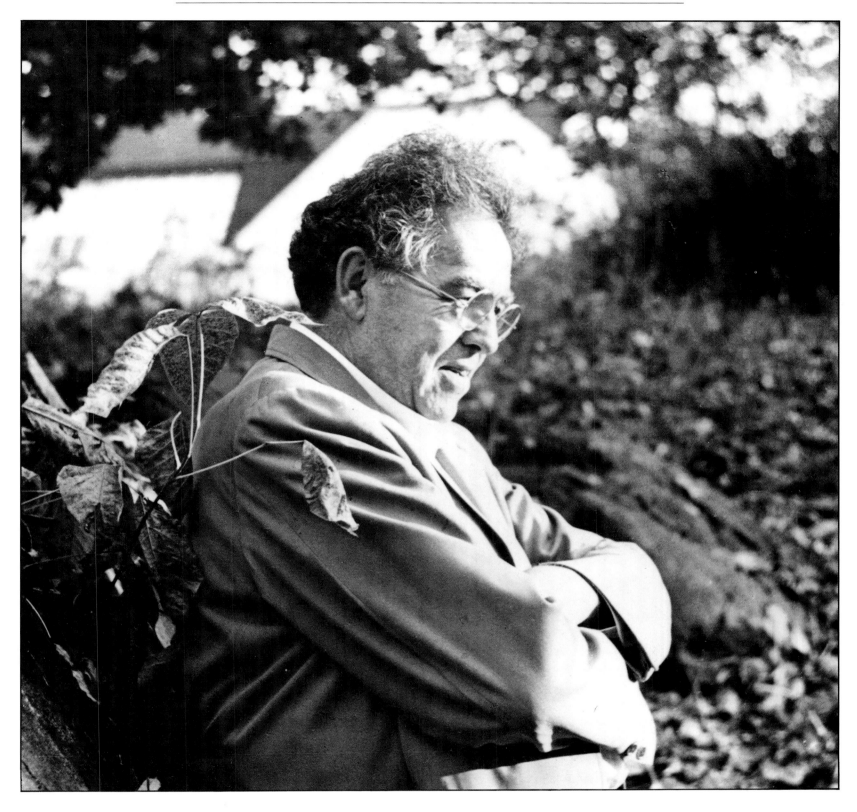

A sad personal event for N.C. Wyeth was the death of his mother on August 11, 1925. She had been a source of comfort and guidance to him and their filial relationship was a close and ardent one. She had been suffering from cancer for a year before her death and her sickness was a very difficult time for Convers.

In his later years, Convers spent more time working on landscape paintings and public murals than his commercial illustrations for publishers. Yet he continued working for some of his publishers. He produced delightful, entertaining canvases for the Houghton Mifflin Company's anthology of children's literature. He also illustrated James Fenimore Cooper's *The Deerslayer* and the cover for the Christmas issue of *The Country Gentleman* featuring Ole St. Nick.

Some of the interesting paintings he was commissioned to furnish for clients as diverse as the Hotel Roosevelt in New York and the Metropolitan Life Insurance Company included a triptych called *Half-Moon in the Hudson* and five murals of Pilgrim scenes. Wyeth painted murals for schools as well, such as *The Giant.*

Wyeth was happiest painting the landscapes around him in Chadds Ford and in Port Clyde. He did several memorable works that were exhibited at the MacBeth Gallery in New York and later at Doll and Richards in Boston. He was aware of the talents of his son Andrew and that he had begun a dynasty of artistry. The conscientious application of observation and technique to painterly goals would continue on in the generations after him. Convers was tragically struck down by a train, in 1945, along with one of his grandsons. Nevertheless, in the masterpieces of Andrew and Andrew's son, James, the gifts of N.C. Wyeth live on today.

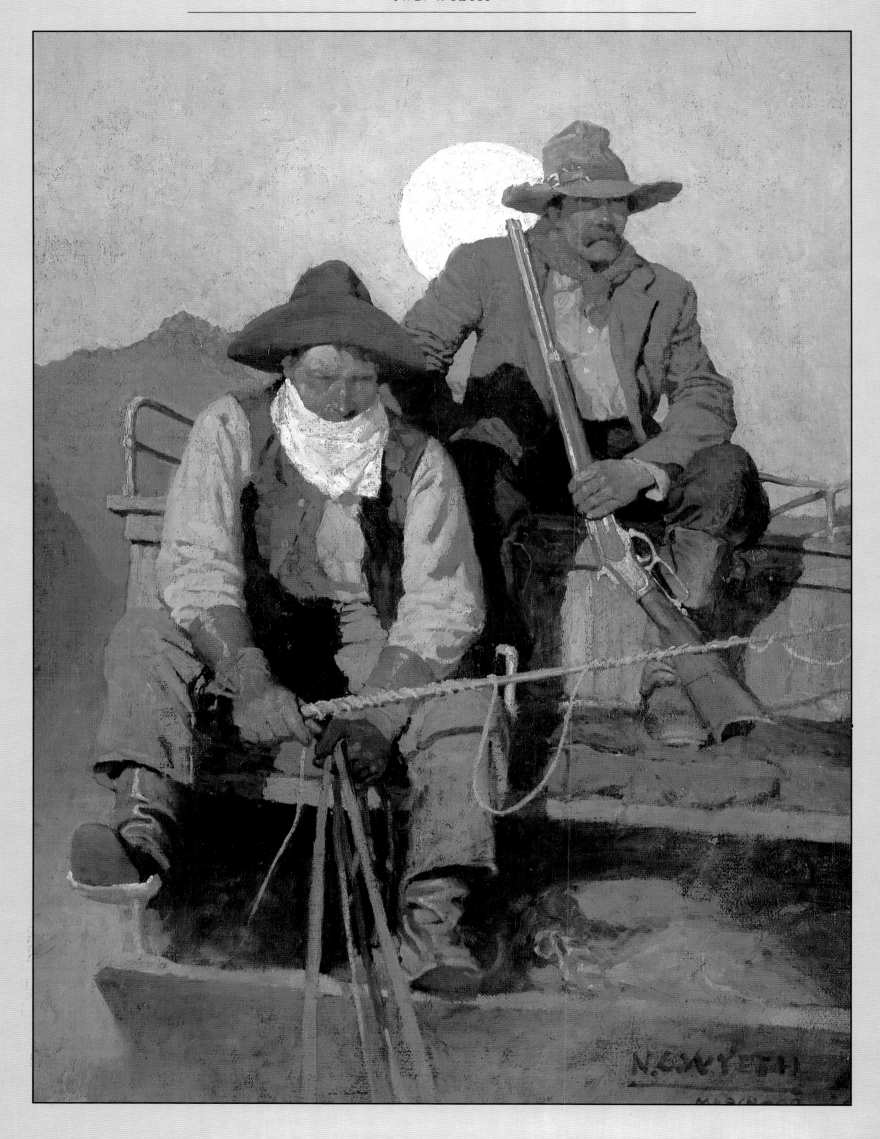

WESTERN ACTION AND SPORTING LIFE

The untamed, wide open territories of the American West and the equally spirited characters who lived there at the turn of the century were the subjects of N.C. Wyeth's earliest published illustrations. The success and enthusiastic public reception of these paintings would engender a continuing series of cowboy and Indian portraits, stagecoach scenes, wagon trains, and trailblazing adventures vividly painted by Wyeth in the ensuing years.

Wyeth made several trips to the West that were sponsored by a variety of national magazines. Although he was familiar with the popular and dramatic western paintings of Frederic Remington, which were on exhibit in New York galleries and museums, he yearned to show the simpler, majestic qualities of these vast and unpopulated Rocky Mountains and the plains that stretched out below them.

Wyeth admired the conviction and dynamic composition of Remington's works but he disliked the artist's emphasis on the horrors of bloody battles and the death and suffering that took place in the West; Wyeth preferred to focus on its intrinsic promise, grandeur, and singular geography.

There was also a special solitude to the West that appealed to Wyeth and he was able to convey this mood in his paintings of shepherds alone with their flocks, cowboys sitting by the camp-fire, and Indians on the trail.

Wyeth had grown up with draft horses and domestic animals on his family's farm in Needham, Massachusetts, but horses played a more vital role in the West. Wyeth's illustrations underscore their value, noble beauty, and strength. On his first trip West, he found employment as a ranch-hand and as a mail carrier, riding many miles between two distant posts. These experiences taught him the necessity of a dependable steed. When his son Andrew later inquired about his ability to draw horses from almost any angle and to render their limbs and expressions accurately, N.C. Wyeth explained that his experience slaughtering a horse out West gave him a memorable lesson in equine anatomy. One feels, though, that it was also his instinctive sympathy and affection for horses, and his familiarity with their conformation that give these paintings a heightened finesse and fidelity.

Wyeth was fascinated by the native tribes of American Indians – including Utes and Navahos – that he met and stayed with on his journeys. He looked forward to each opportunity to draw them and learn their customs. He frequently bartered with them to obtain articles of clothing, blankets, headdresses, beaded moccasins, and decorated quirts (braided riding whips) that he could use to set up still lifes back at his studio.

The hours he spent studying and sketching their faces and watching and participating in their daily routines provided him with a storehouse of visual images for his future canvases. In many of his later paintings, he adapted their environs to suit a particular theme. Though the new settings were woodlands, lakes, and mountain streams, the figures hearken back to the Indians he had lived among in the West.

The offers for his western illustrations were abundant from the beginning of his career. N.C. Wyeth's pictures convey both the rich color of the surroundings and the striking events and wondrous encounters that occurred between man and nature and often, between man and man.

Left:
The Pay Stage, 1909
Scribner's Magazine, August 1910
Oil on canvas, 38 × 26½ in.
Collection of First Interstate Bank of Arizona, N.A, Phoenix, AZ

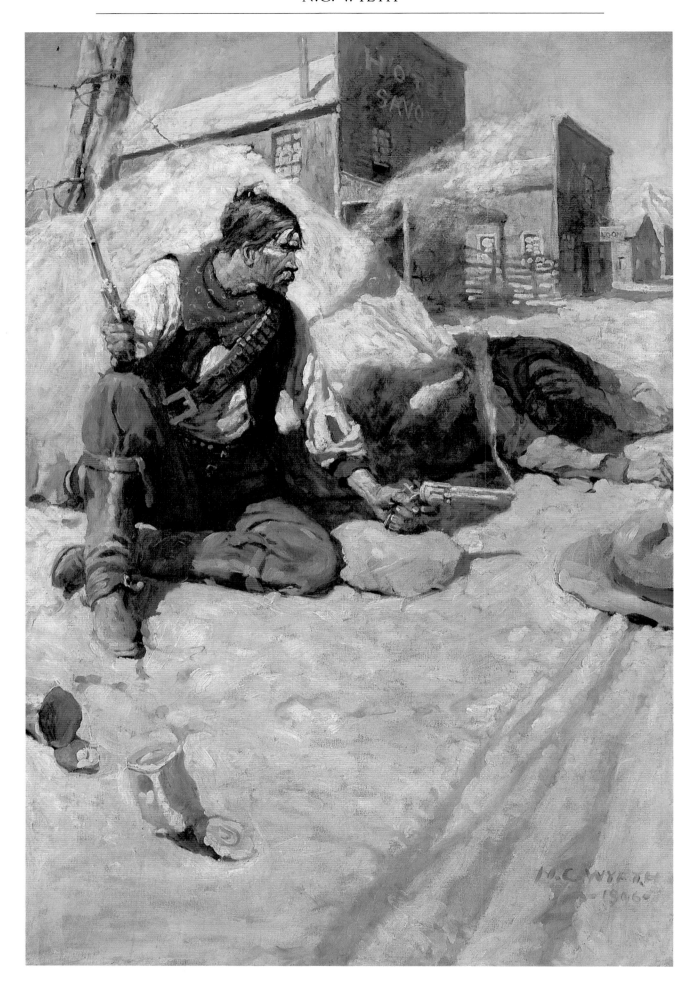

**Sitting up cross-legged, with each hand holding a gun
from which came thin wisps of smoke,** 1906
"Bar 20 Range Yarns" by Clarence Edward Mulford
Outing Magazine, May 1906
Oil on canvas, 37 × 26 in.
Collection of First Interstate Bank of Arizona, N.A, Phoenix, AZ

Right:
**Above the Sea of Round, Shiny Backs the Thin Loops
Swirled and Shot into Volumes of Dust,** 1904
Oil on canvas, 38¼ × 26 in.
Gift of John M. Schiff
Buffalo Bill Historical Center, Cody, WY

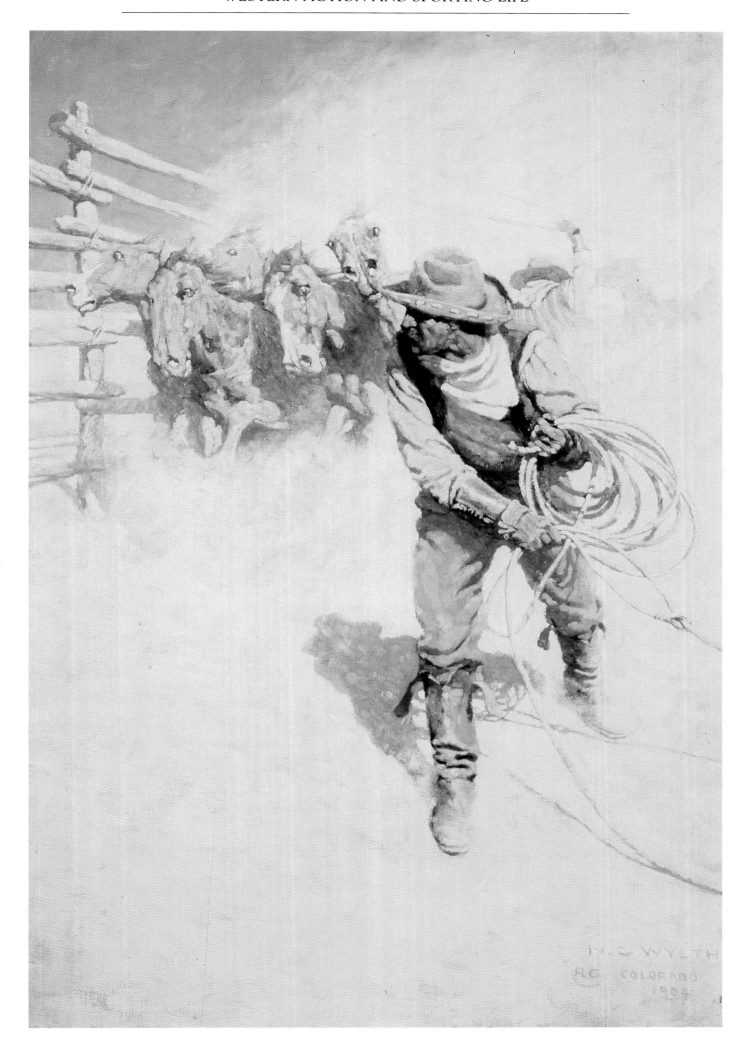

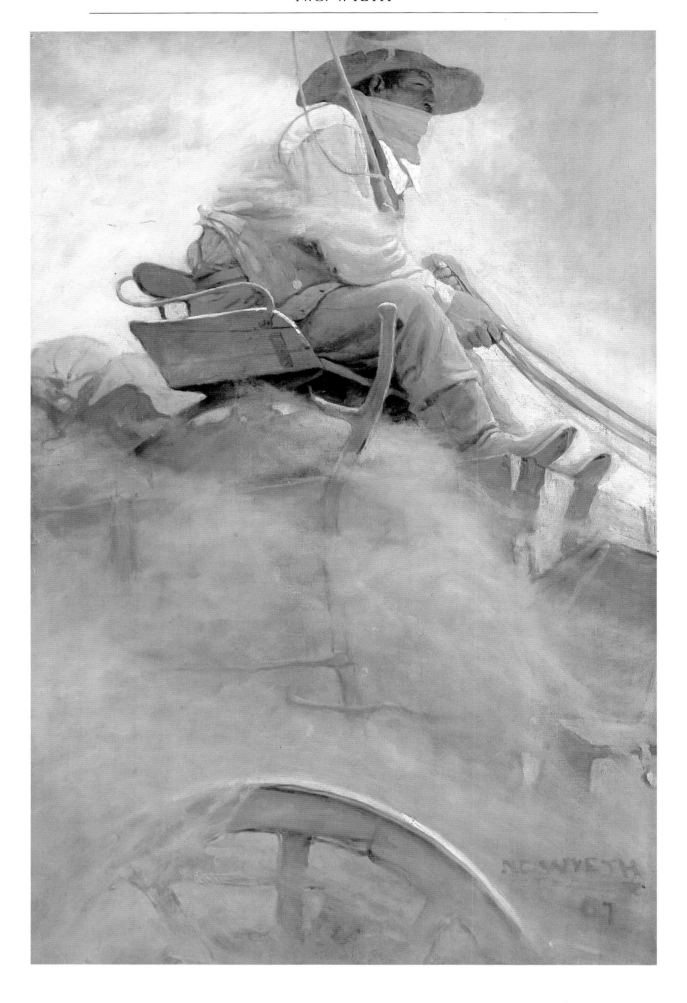

The Ore Wagon, 1907
"The Misadventures of Cassidy" by Edward S. Moffat
McClure's Magazine, May 1908
Oil on canvas, 38 × 25 in.
Collection of First Interstate Bank of Arizona, N.A, Phoenix, AZ

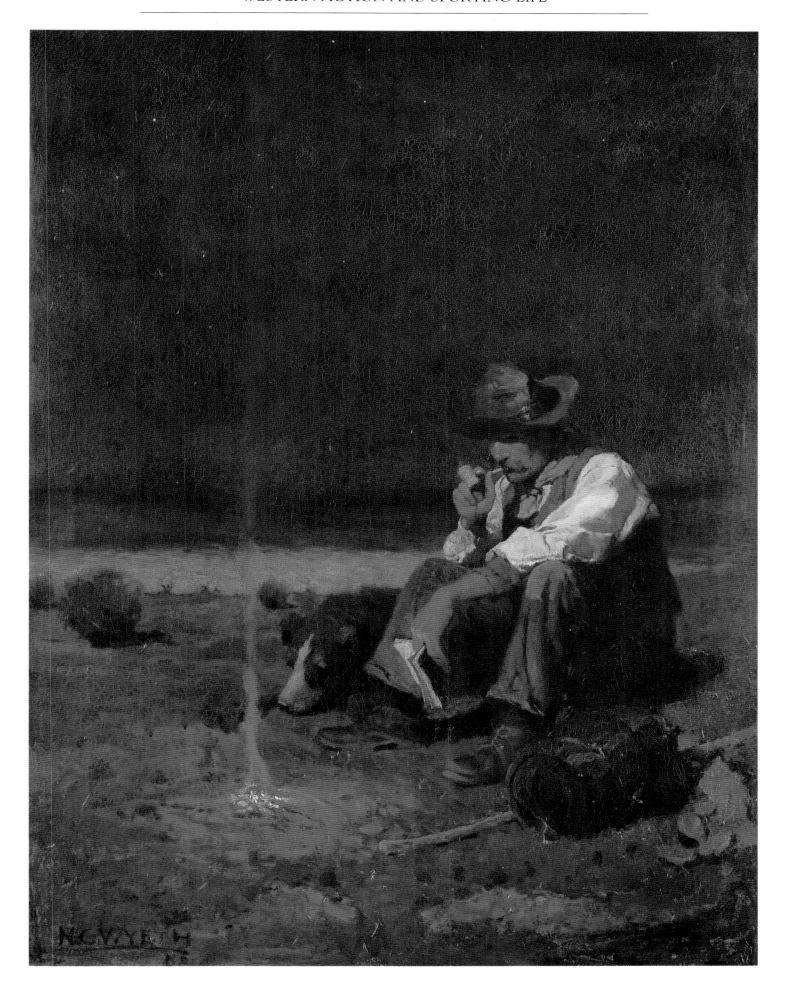

The Plains Herder, 1908
"A Sheep-Herder of the South-West" by N. C. Wyeth
Scribner's Magazine, January 1909
Oil on canvas, 37⅛ × 28⅛ in.
Collection of First Interstate Bank of Arizona, N.A, Phoenix, AZ

Overleaf:
Mexican Shepherd, 1908
"A Sheep-Herder of the South-West" by N. C. Wyeth
Scribner's Magazine, January 1909
Oil on canvas, 28⅛ × 37¼ in.
Collection of First Interstate Bank of Arizona, N.A, Phoenix, AZ

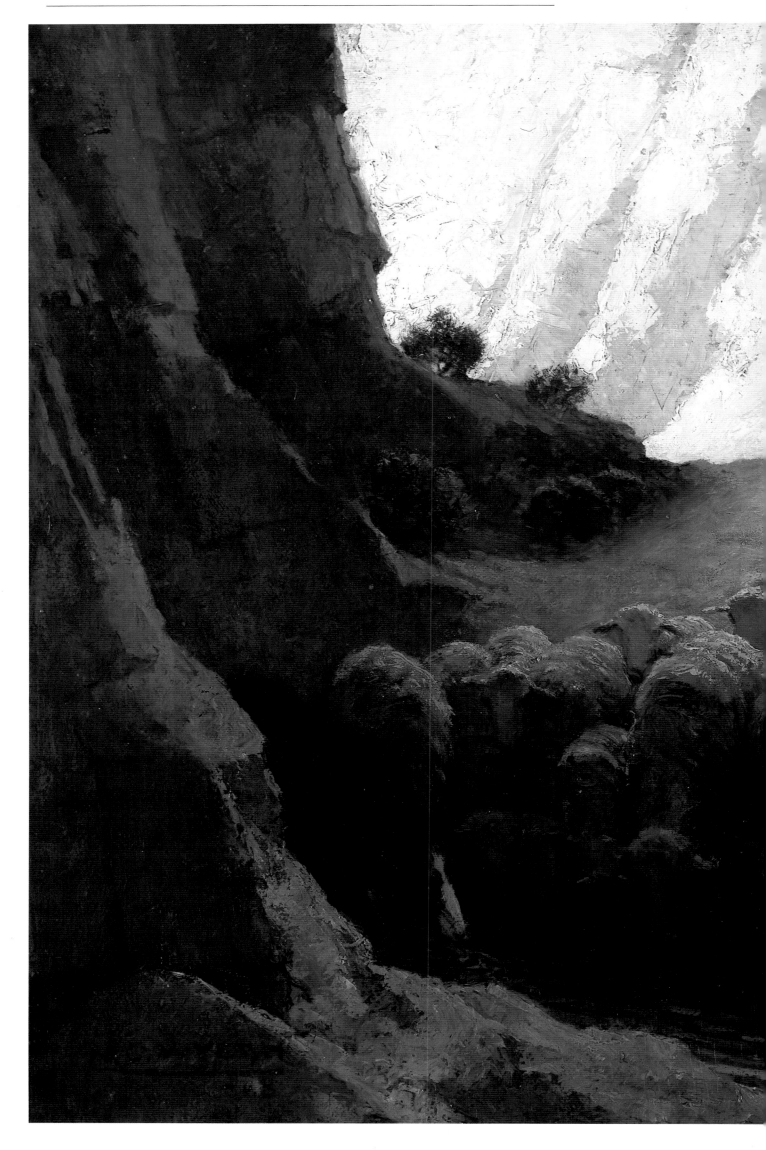

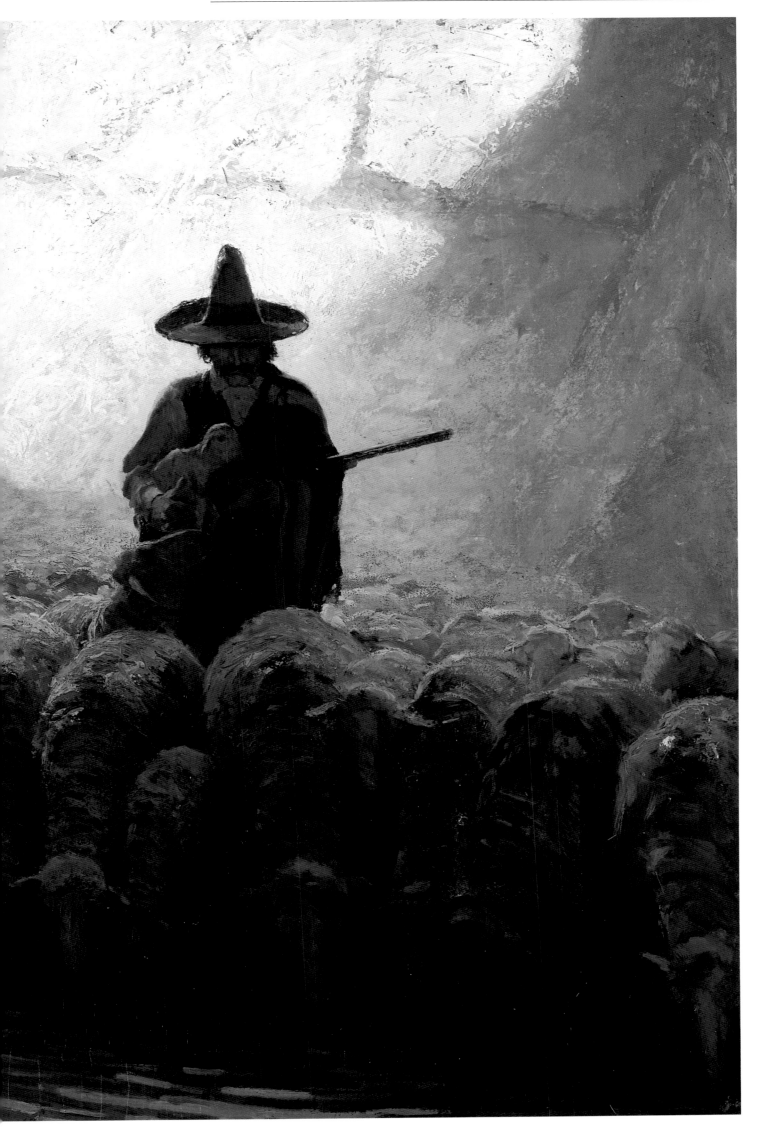

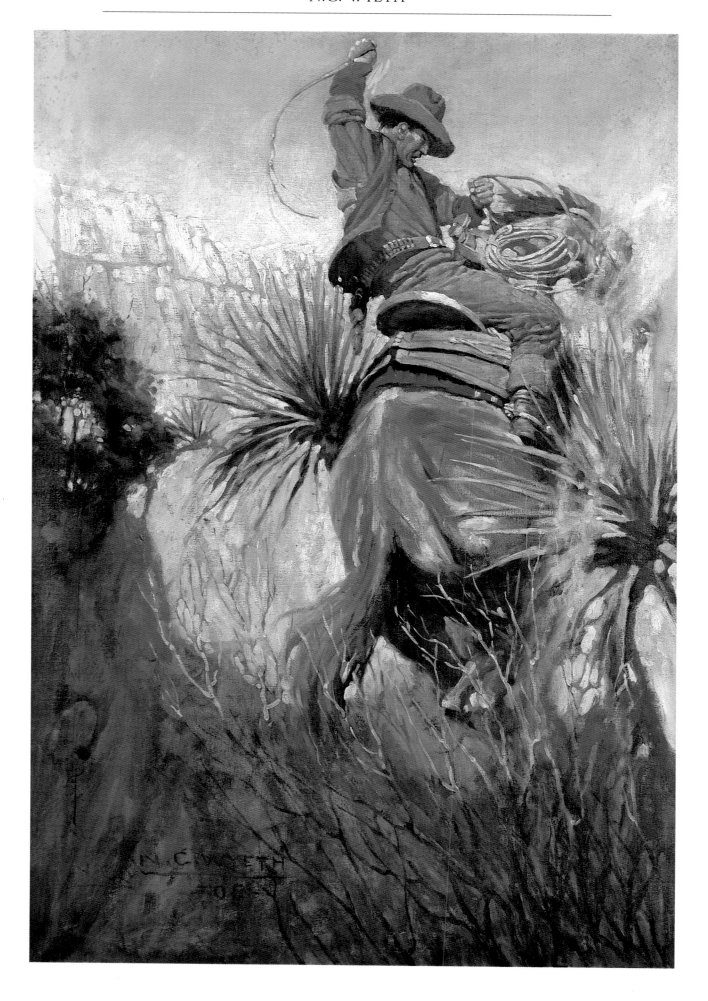

I Saw His Horse Jump Back Dodgin' a Rattlesnake or Somethin', 1905
"Arizona Nights" by Stewart Edward White
McClure's Magazine, April 1906
Oil on canvas, 36 × 23¾ in.
Collection of First Interstate Bank of Arizona, N.A, Phoenix, AZ

Right:
The Admirable Outlaw (My English Friend Thought It Was a Hold-up), 1906
"The Admirable Outlaw" by M'Cready Sykes
Scribner's Magazine, November 1906
Oil on canvas, 38 × 23⅝ in.
Courtesy of the National Cowboy Hall of Fame and Western Heritage Center, Oklahoma City, OK

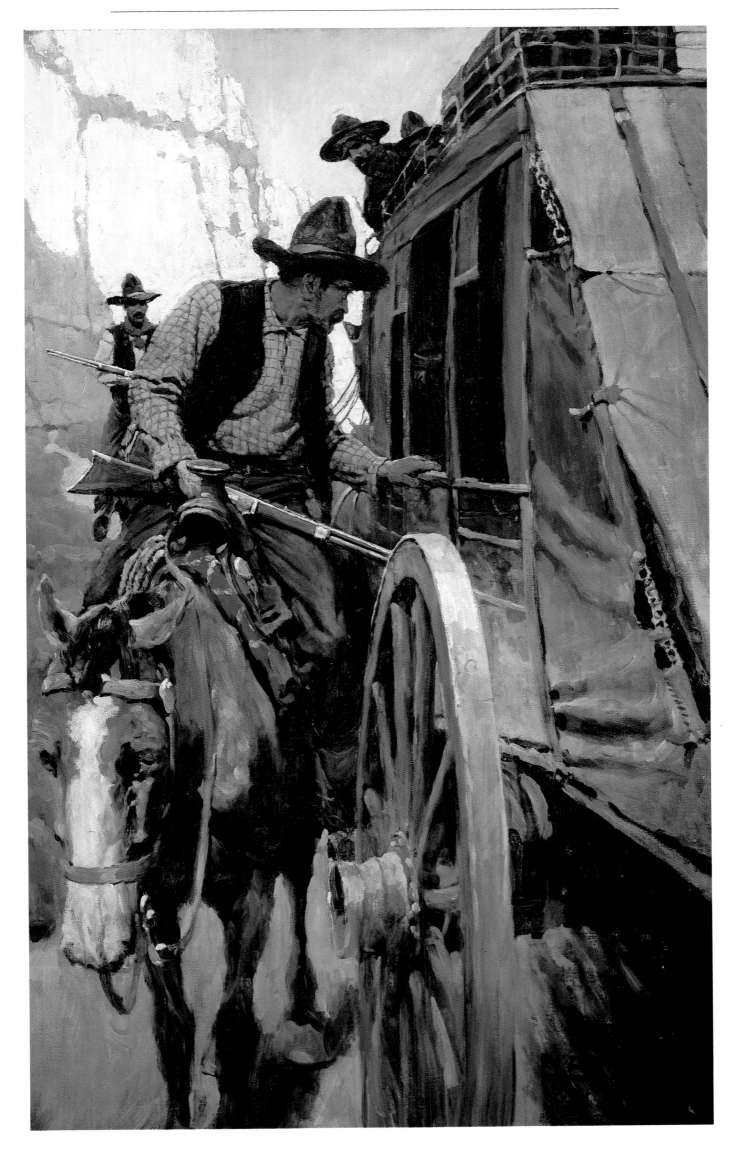

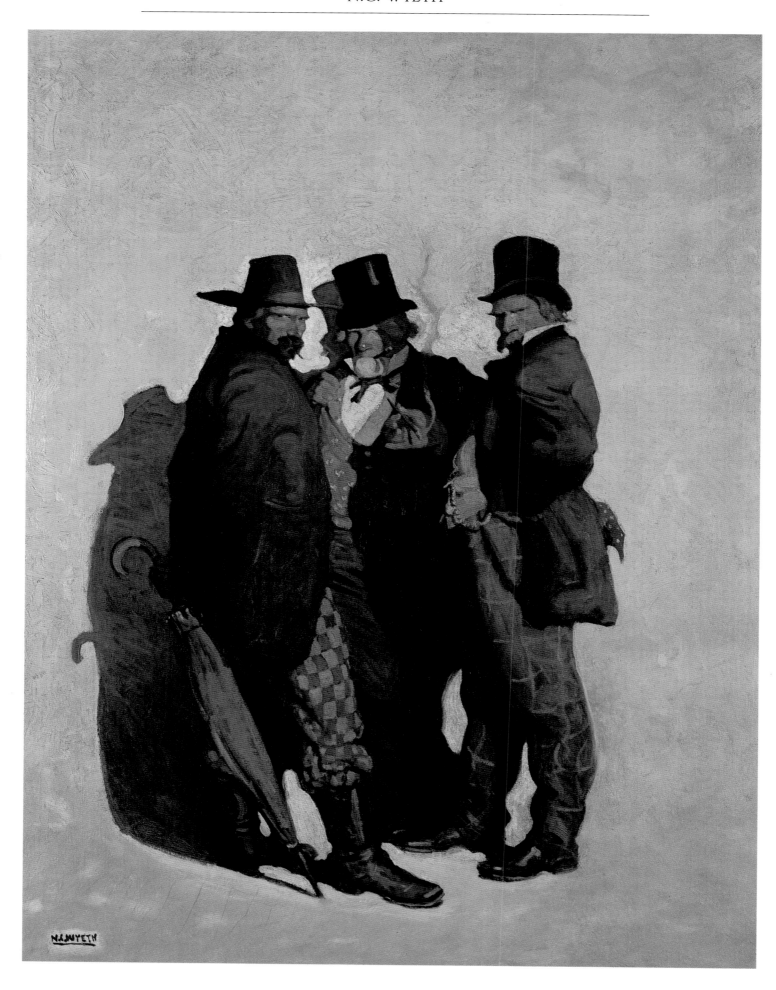

The Carpetbaggers, c. 1912
Cover, *The Pike County Ballads* by John Hay
Houghton Mifflin Company, Boston, 1912
Oil on canvas, 49 × 38 in.
Collected by C. T. and Claire McLaughlin
Diamond M Foundation Fine Art Collection, Lubbock, TX
Photography by Nicky Olson

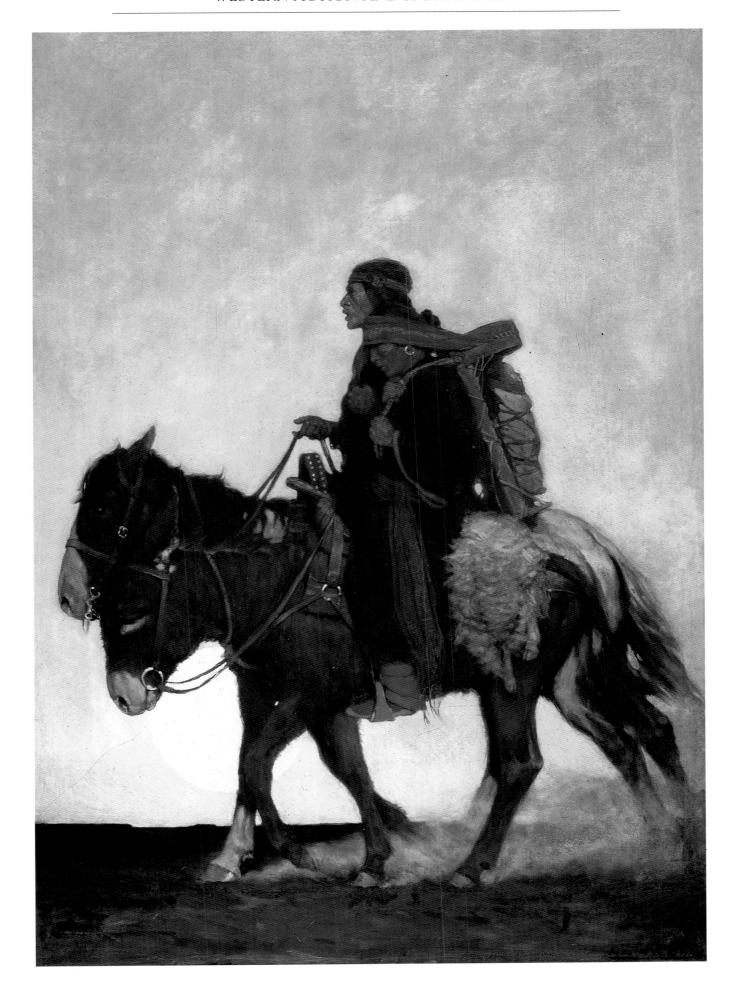

On the October Trail, 1908
Frontispiece, *Scribner's Magazine,* October 1908
Oil on canvas, 41¾ × 29¼ in.
Collection of the Brandywine River Museum
Photography by Peter Ralston

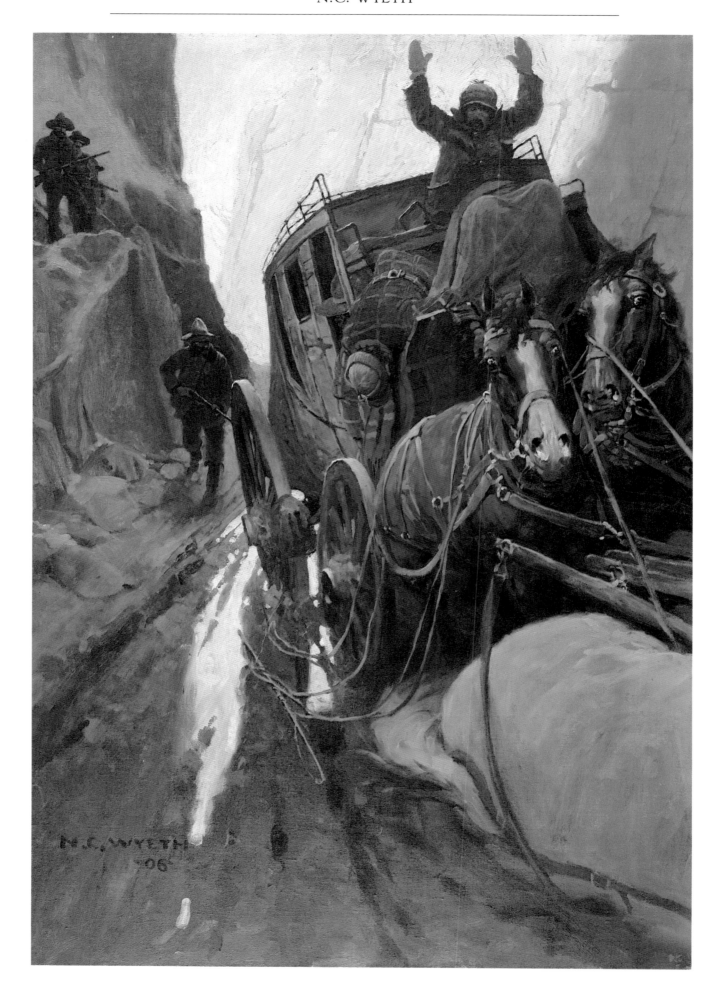

Hands Up, 1906
"The Story of Montana" by C. P. Connolly
McClure's Magazine, August 1906
Oil on canvas, 43 × 30 in.
Courtesy of Valley National Bank, Phoenix, AZ

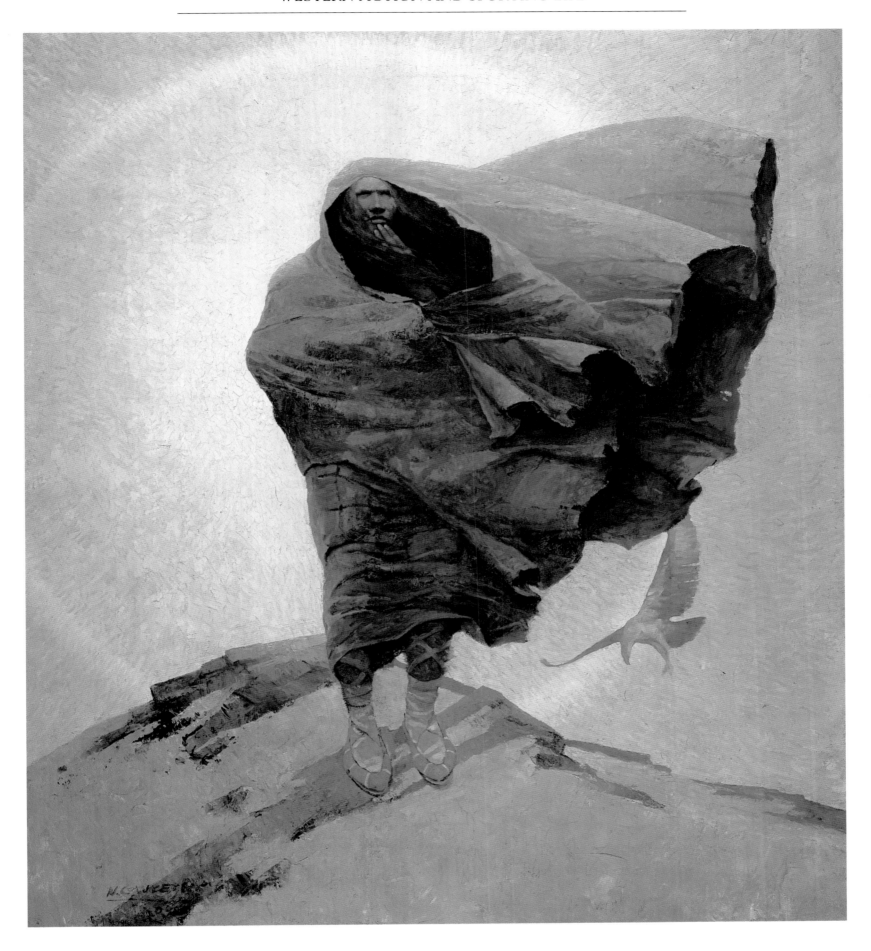

Winter. "Death," 1909
"The Moods" by George T. Marsh
Scribner's Magazine, December 1909
Oil on canvas, 33 × 30 in.
Collection of Mr. and Mrs. Andrew Wyeth
Photograph courtesy of the Brandywine River Museum
Photography by Peter Ralston

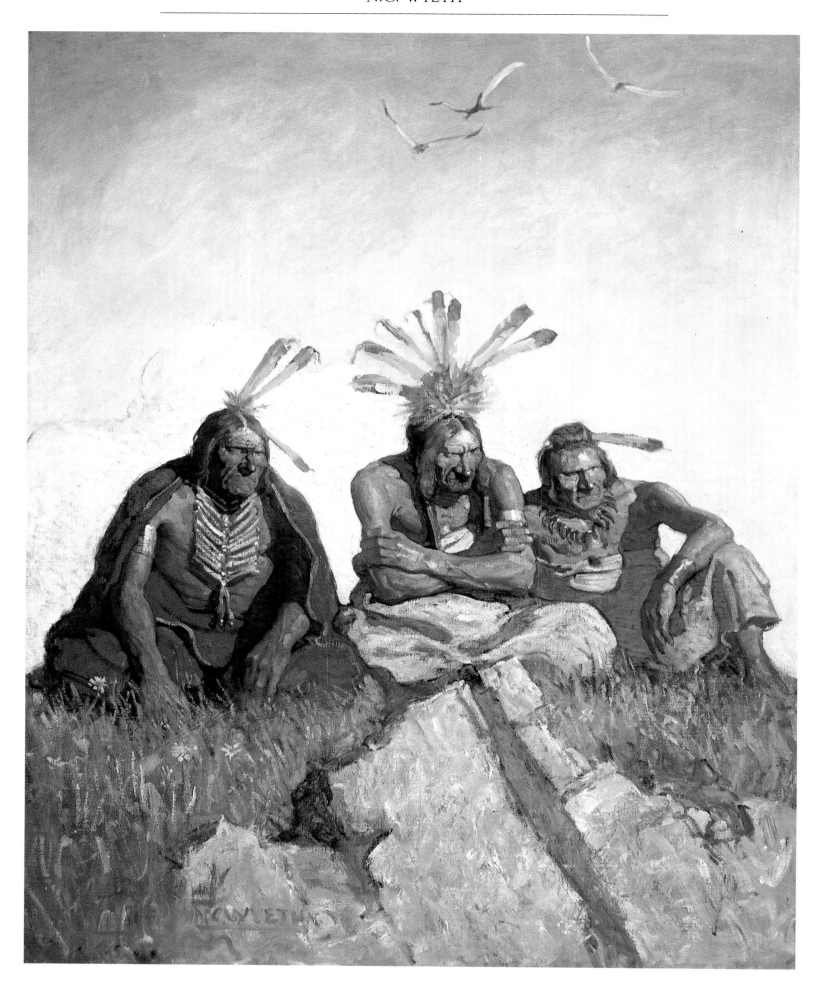

Nothing would escape their black, jewel-like inscrutable eyes, 1911
"Growing Up" by Gouverneur Morris
Harper's Monthly Magazine, November 1911
Oil on canvas, 6¾ × 37⅞ in.
The Warner Collection of Gulf States Paper Corporation, Tuscaloosa, AL

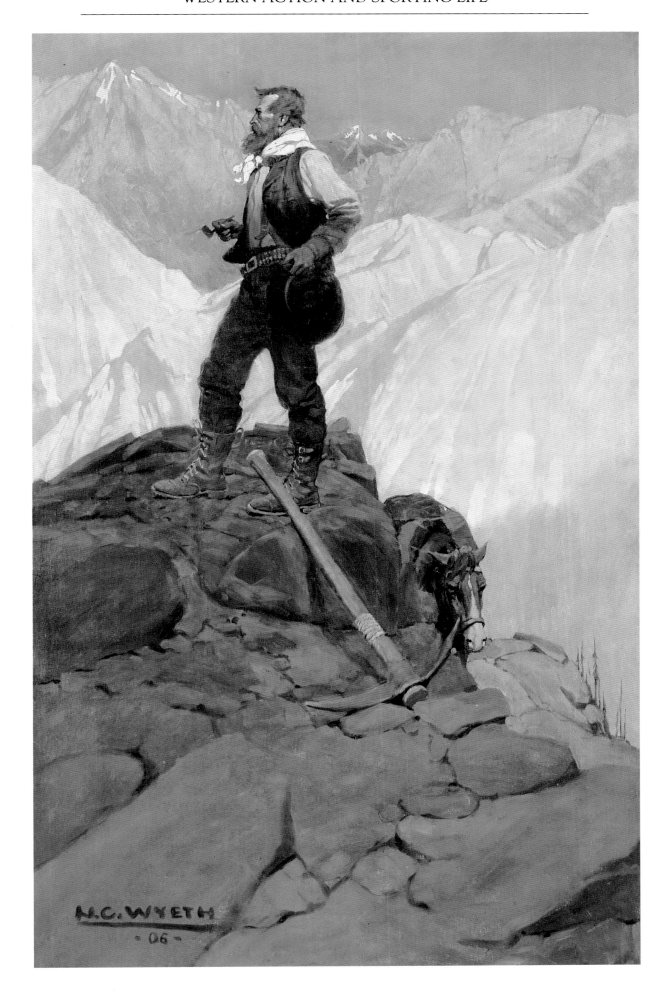

The Prospector, 1906
"The Story of Montana" by C. P. Connolly
McClure's Magazine, September 1906
Oil on canvas, 47 × 29¾ in.
Collection of First Interstate Bank of Arizona, N.A.

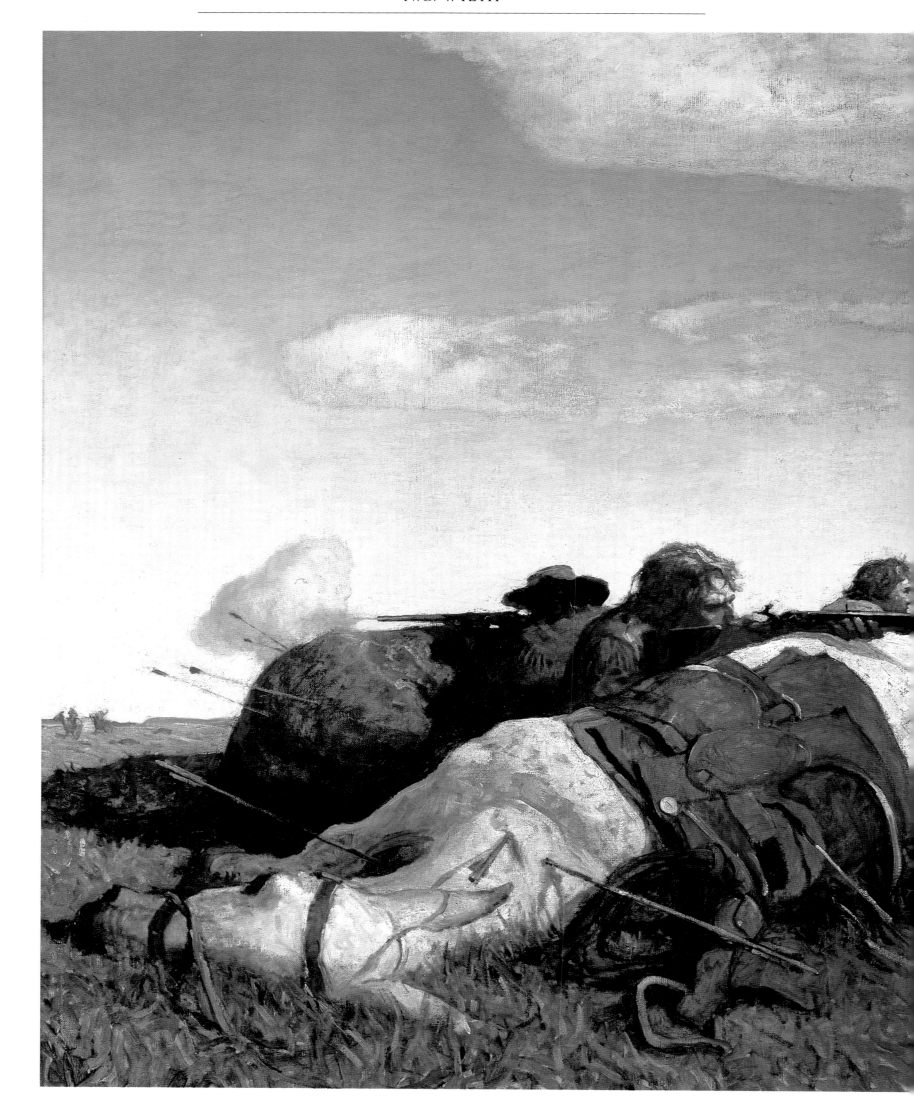

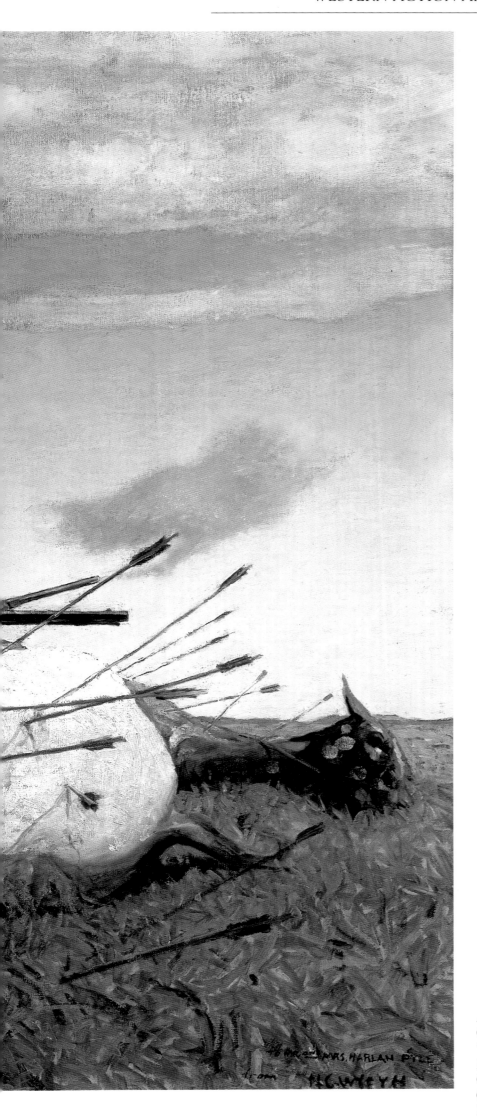

**A Shower of Arrows Rained on Our Dead Horses From the
Closing Circle of Red-Men ("Fight on the Plains"),** 1916
"The Great West That Was" by Col. William F. Cody
Hearst's Magazine, 1916
Oil on canvas, 32⅜ × 40⅜ in.
Collection of Mr. and Mrs. Andrew Wyeth
Photograph courtesy of the Brandywine River Museum, Chadds Ford, PA
Photography by Peter Ralston

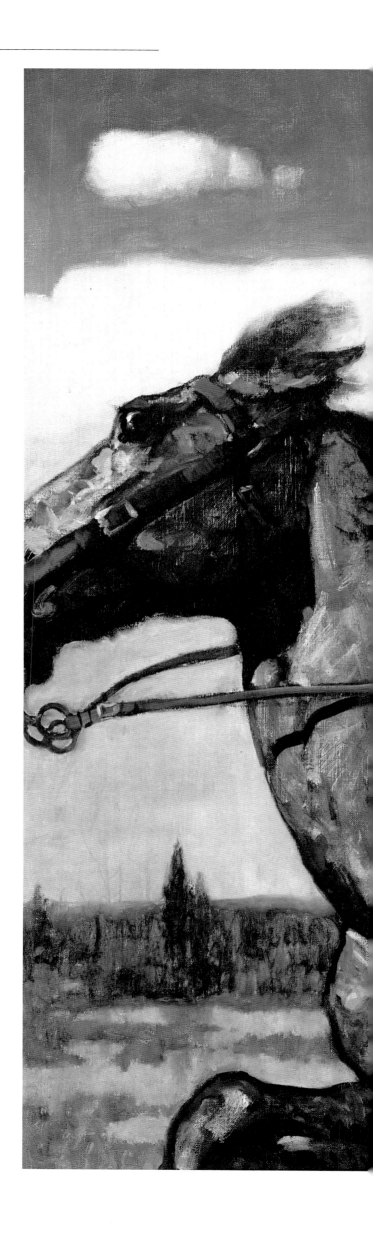

Buffalo Swamp, 1923
"Buffalo Swamp, A Ballad of the Moonshine Belt" by Damon Runyon
Hearst's International Magazine, June 1923
Oil on canvas, 34 × 38 in.
Gene Autry Western Heritage Museum, Los Angeles, CA

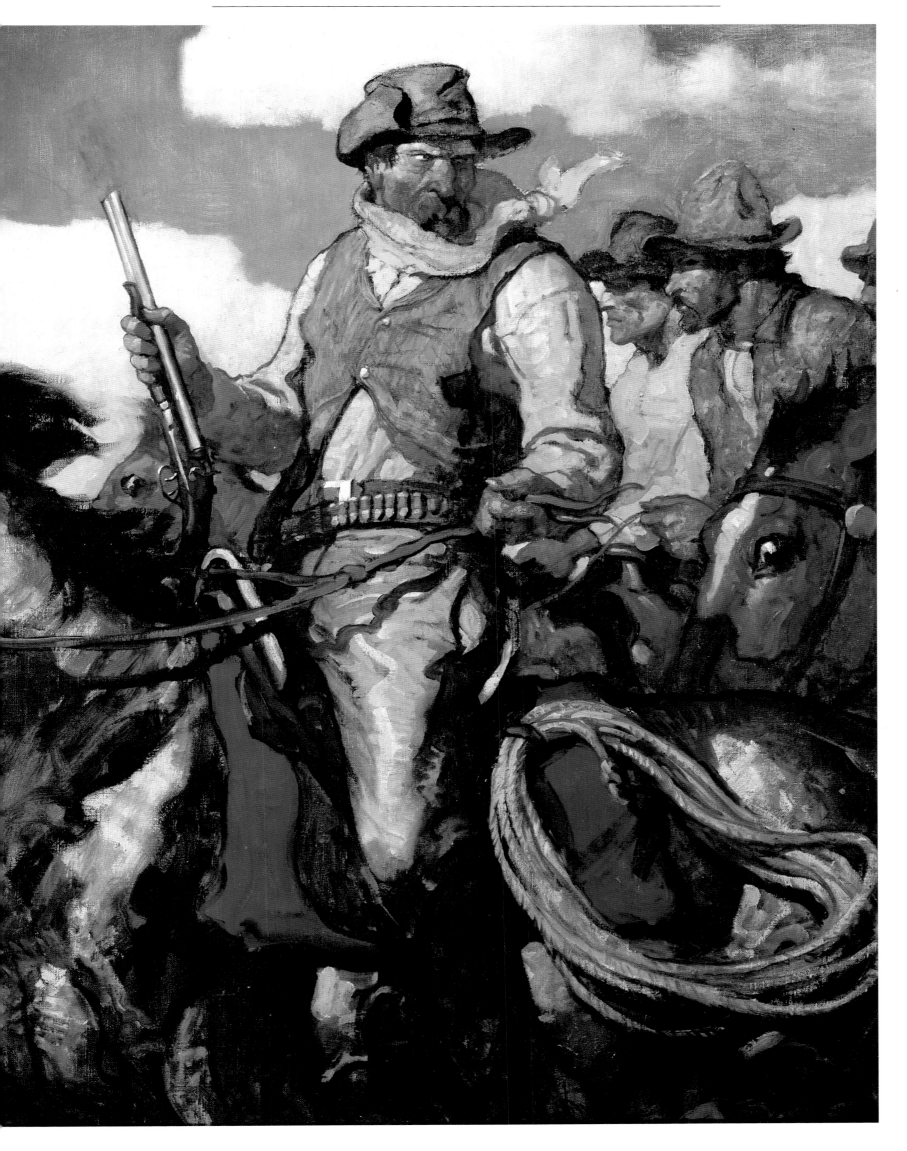

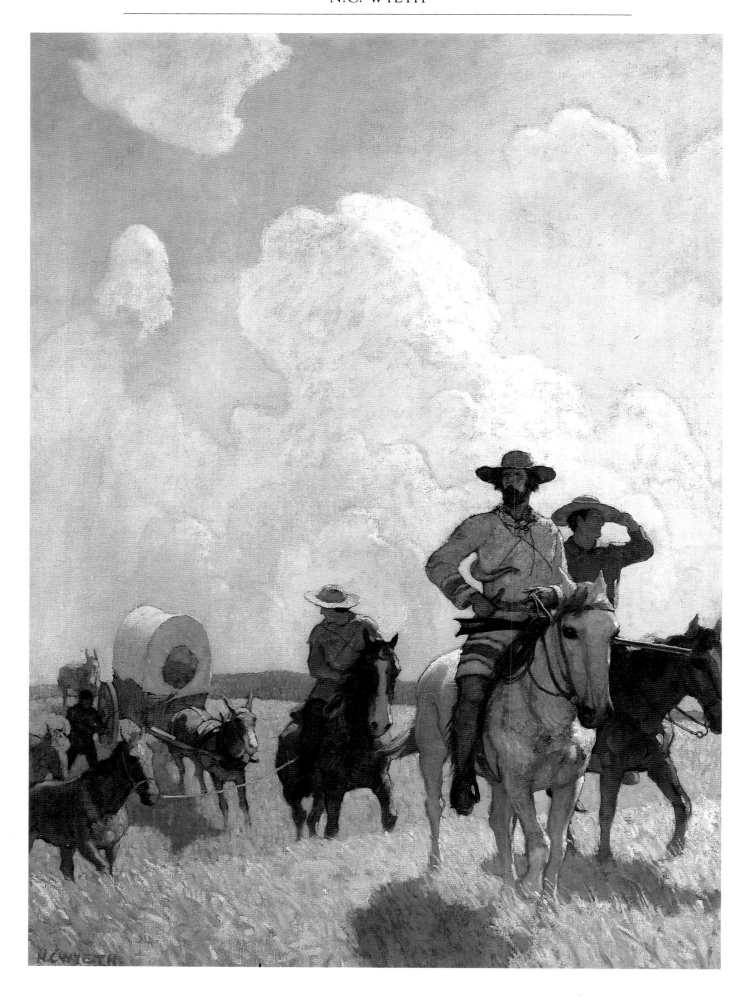

**The Parkman Outfit – Henry Chatillon,
Guide and Hunter,** c. 1925
The Oregon Trail by Francis Parkman
Little, Brown and Company, 1925
Oil on canvas, 40½ × 29⅛ in.
Collection of First Interstate Bank of Arizona, N.A, Phoenix, AZ

Right:
Francis Parkman, c. 1925
Frontispiece, *The Oregon Trail* by Francis Parkman
Little, Brown and Company, 1925
Oil on canvas, 40 × 28 in.
*Courtesy of the National Cowboy Hall of Fame and
Western Heritage Center, Oklahoma City, OK*

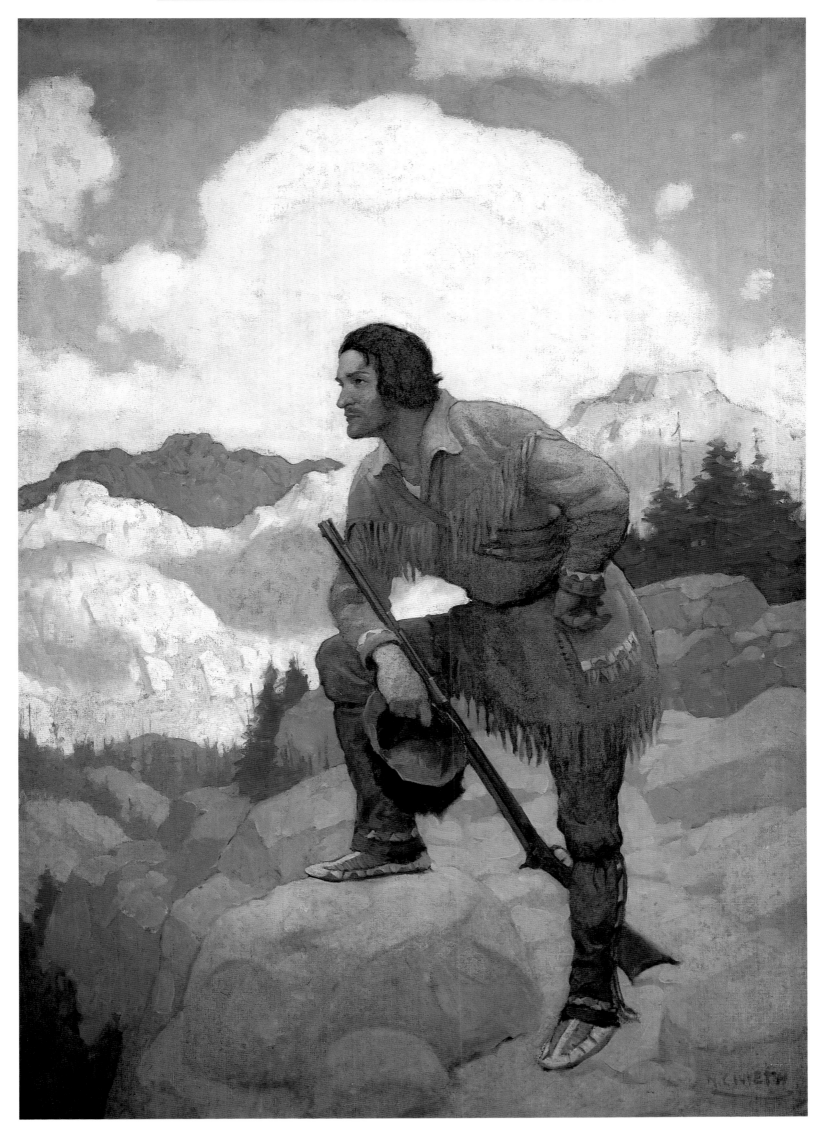

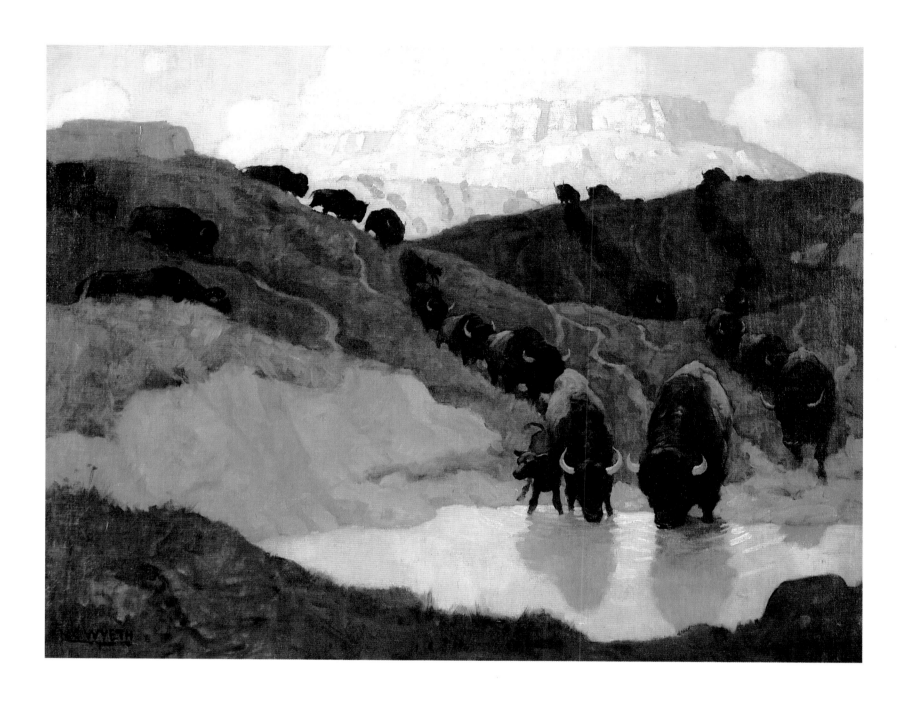

The Water-Hole, c. 1925
Endpapers, *The Oregon Trail* by Francis Parkman
Little, Brown and Company, 1925
Oil on canvas, 28 × 36 in.
Collection of First Interstate Bank of Arizona, N.A, Phoenix, AZ

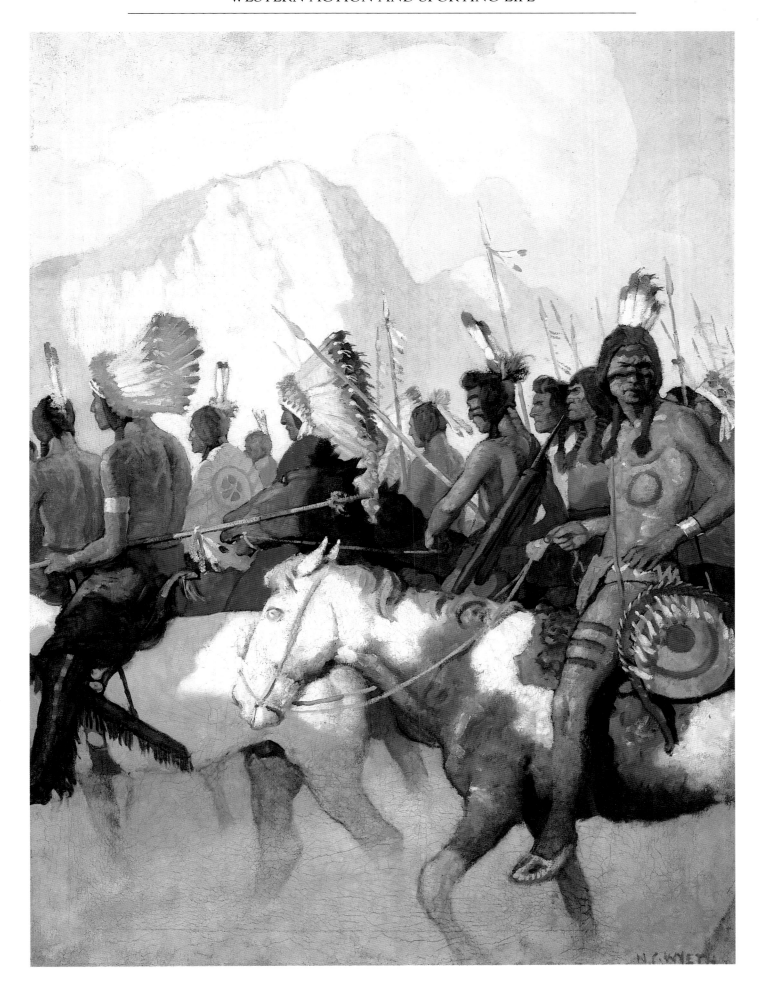

An Indian War Party, c. 1925
The Oregon Trail by Francis Parkman
Little, Brown and Company, 1925
Oil on canvas, 38⅝ × 28 in.
Gene Autry Western Heritage Museum, Los Angeles, CA

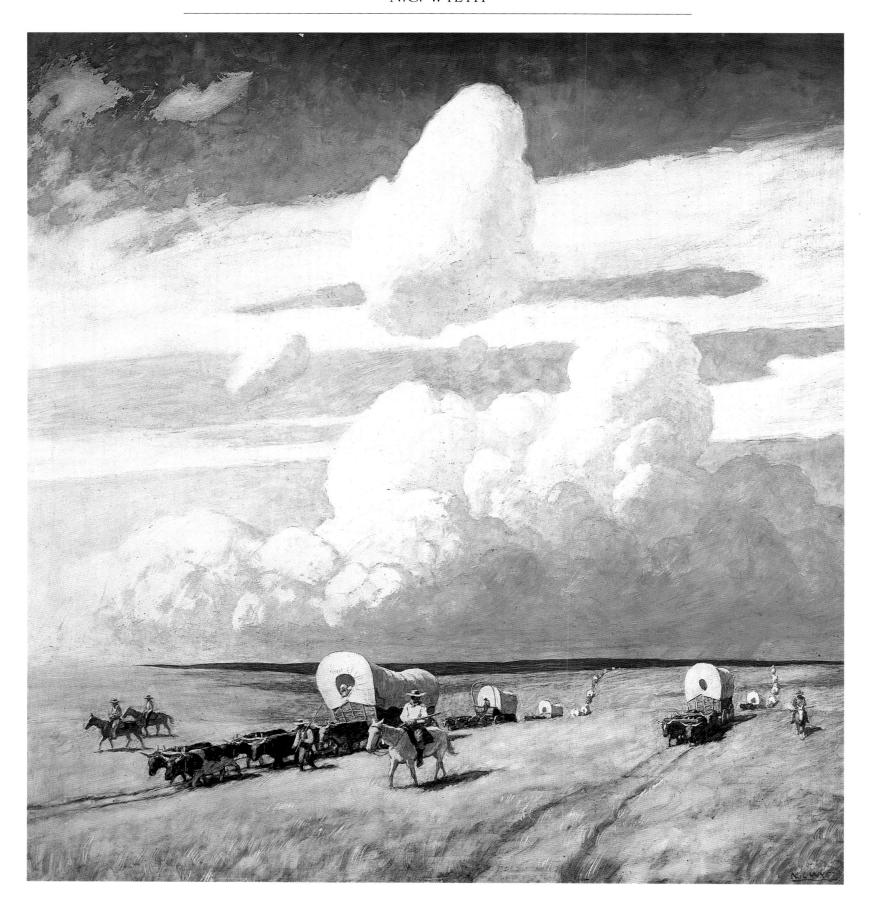

Covered Wagons, 1940
Calendar illustration
Oil with some tempera on panel, 26⅛ × 24½ in.
Gift of John Morrell & Company, 1940
From the University Art Collection, Iowa State University, Ames, IA

Right:
Cowboy Watering His Horse, c. 1937
Oil on masonite, 36 × 24 in.
Museum of Texas Tech University, Lubbock, TX
Photography by Nicky Olson

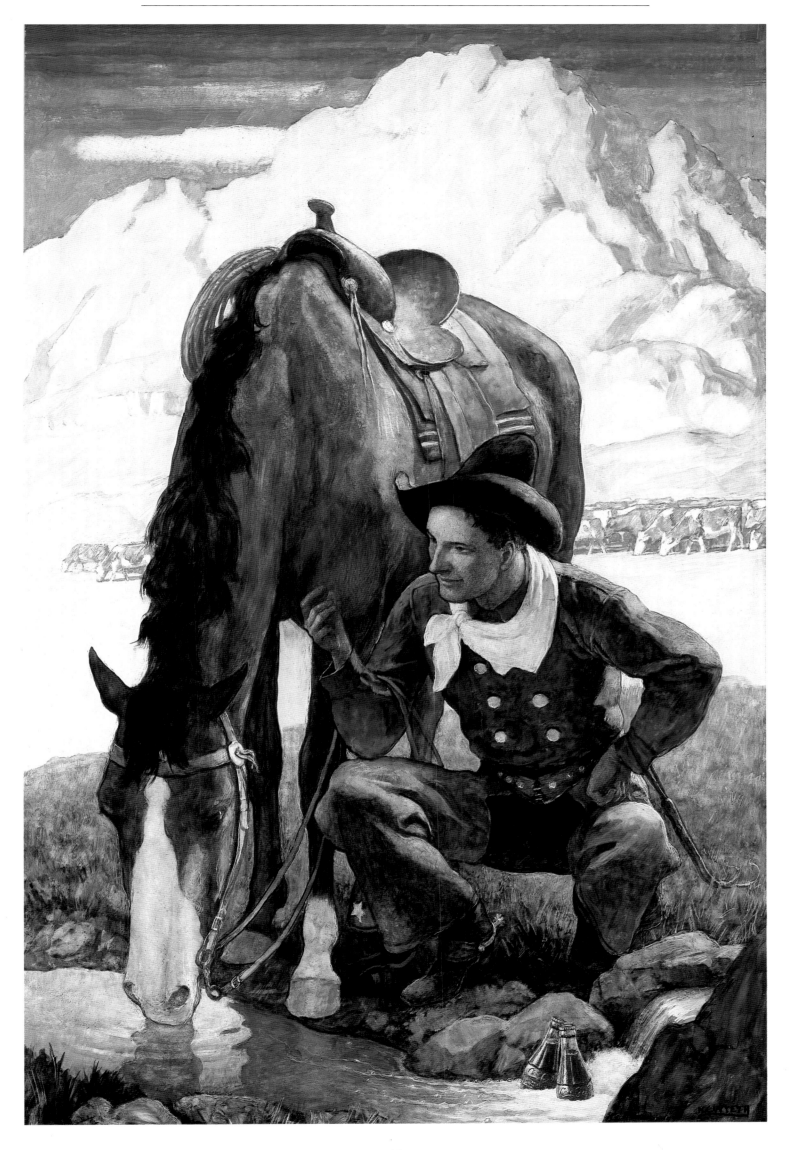

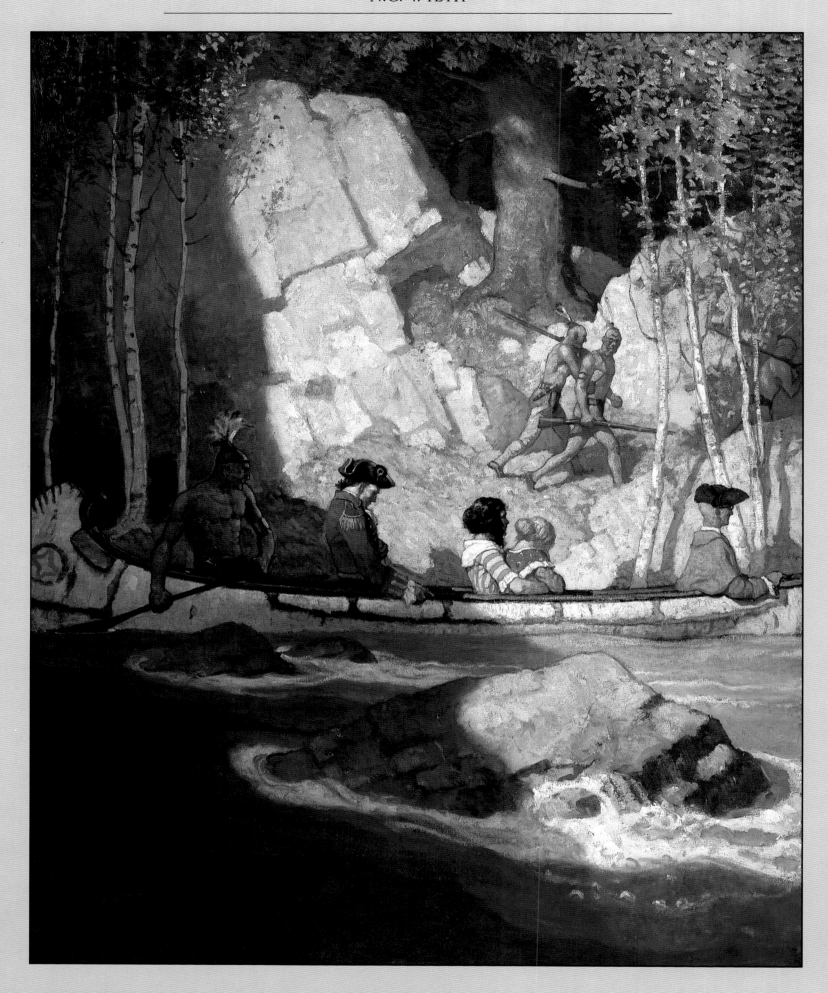

The Captives, 1919
The Last of the Mohicans by James Fenimore Cooper
Charles Scribner's Sons, 1919
Private Collection
Photography by Peter Ralston

Book and Magazine Illustrations

N.C. Wyeth is best known for the superb illustrations he painted to accompany the text of many childrens' classics, tales of adventure, historic and patriotic poems, and magazine stories. He worked during the golden years of magazine illustration before photography became the medium of choice for advertisers. The quality of his paintings was such that as recently as 1981, a revised edition of Robert Louis Stevenson's *Treasure Island* carried his original illustrations.

Among the many well-known authors whose publishers commissioned Wyeth to illustrate their novels and books were Mark Twain, Robert Louis Stevenson, James Fenimore Cooper, Arthur Conan Doyle, Daniel DeFoe, Marjorie Kinnan Rawlings, and Henry David Thoreau. One could admire his glorious, virile brushwork in books as diverse as Jules Verne's *The Mysterious Island*, James Fenimore Cooper's *Last of the Mohicans,* and Marjorie Kinnan Rawlings's *The Yearling.*

Wyeth worked quickly and often would complete a canvas in one morning. This enabled him to satisfy the commercial requirements of both magazine editors and publishing companies. Yet he often had grave doubts about the value of such paintings he could produce so readily. He longed to compose his own designs free from the pressures of adapting his style to suit the public taste. Nevertheless, what he was able to accomplish seems astounding by today's standards, especially considering that he painted full-scale canvases for many of his illustrations, which were then reduced for reproduction.

N.C. Wyeth traveled often within the United States to research the background and distinguishing geographical character of many of the novels. He journeyed to the Adirondack Mountains to learn more about the scenery there for his Indian paintings in *Last of the Mohicans.* He visited the hot and humid tropical everglades in Florida to more accurately portray this region for Marjorie Kinnan Rawlings's *The Yearling.* He stayed at the Homestead Inn in Warm Springs, Virginia, and went to Civil War battle sites so that his paintings for Mary Johnston's *The Long Roll* and *Cease Firing* would reflect these locations.

Wyeth used the places, people, and houses he recalled from his youth to furnish the subject matter of his illustrations. The Admiral Benbow Inn featured in the painting of *Old Pew* in *Treasure Island* was based on his childhood home in Needham, Massachusetts. The facial characteristics and demeanor of Rip Van Winkle in the story by Washington Irving were closely modeled on an elderly gentleman named Mr. Onion, whom Wyeth remembered from his youth. The fields, trees, hills, and skies in many of his illustrations are very similar to those in Chadds Ford.

N.C. Wyeth learned his craft from Howard Pyle who organized a school of illustration in Wilmington, Delaware, at the turn of the century. Students of Pyle appeared in all of the popular magazines of this era, including *McClure's, Scribner's, Outing Magazine, Century* and *Colliers.* Wyeth himself taught a small group of students, including his son Andrew and daughter Henriette, in his studio in Chadds Ford. He also wrote a number of instructive articles about his methods and techniques.

The advice he proffered in one such newspaper piece that appeared in the October 13, 1912, issue of *The New York Times* gives one an insight into his strategies and the theory of his mentor as well. "The ability to select subject matter is an art in itself and calls to action similar dramatic instincts required in the staging of a play. By avoiding the shackles of explicit action and detail the illustrator will find a field of far greater range upon which to exercise his powers."

N.C. Wyeth's book and magazine illustrations are riveting, dramatic, and resourceful, rendered with such a sure hand they continue to please viewers today.

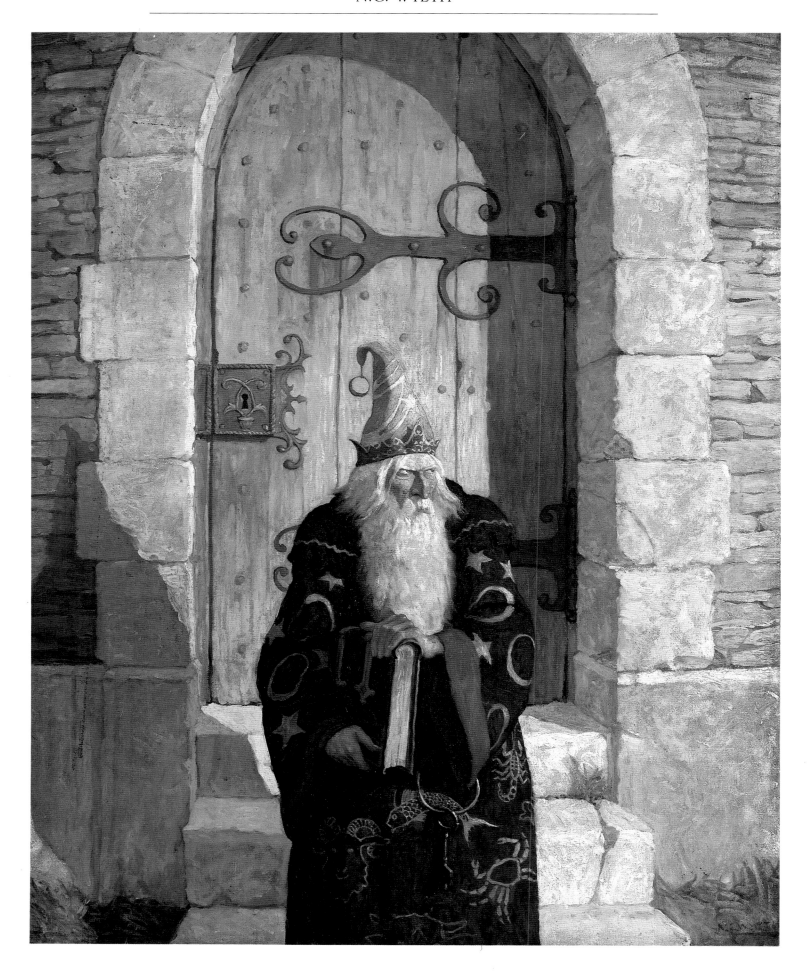

The Astrologer (On the Fourth Day Comes the Astrologer from His Crumbling Old Tower), 1916
The Mysterious Stranger by Mark Twain
Harper and Brothers, Publishers, 1916
Oil on canvas, 40 × 32 in.
Collected by C. T. and Claire McLaughlin
Diamond M. Foundation Fine Art Collection, Lubbock, TX
Photography by Nicky Olson

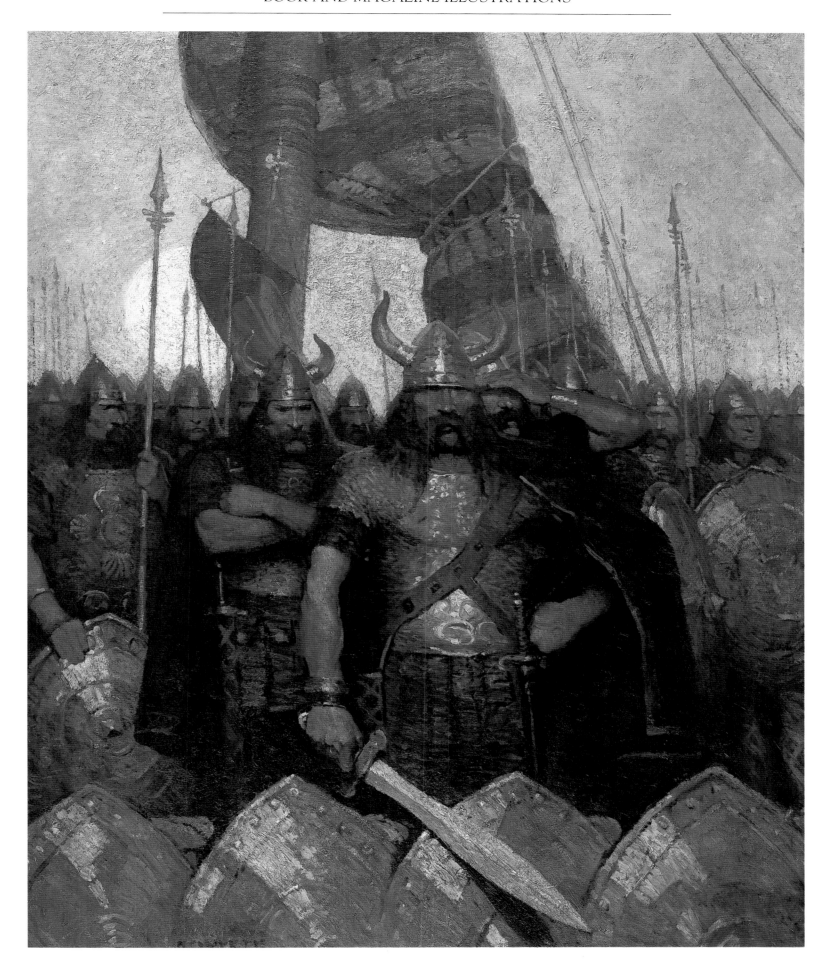

The First Cargo, 1910
"Through the Mists II: The First Cargo"
by Sir Arthur Conan Doyle
Scribner's Magazine, December 1910
Oil on canvas
Collection of the New York Public Library, Central Children's Room,
Donnell Library Center, New York, NY
Photograph courtesy of the Brandywine River Museum
Photography by Peter Ralston

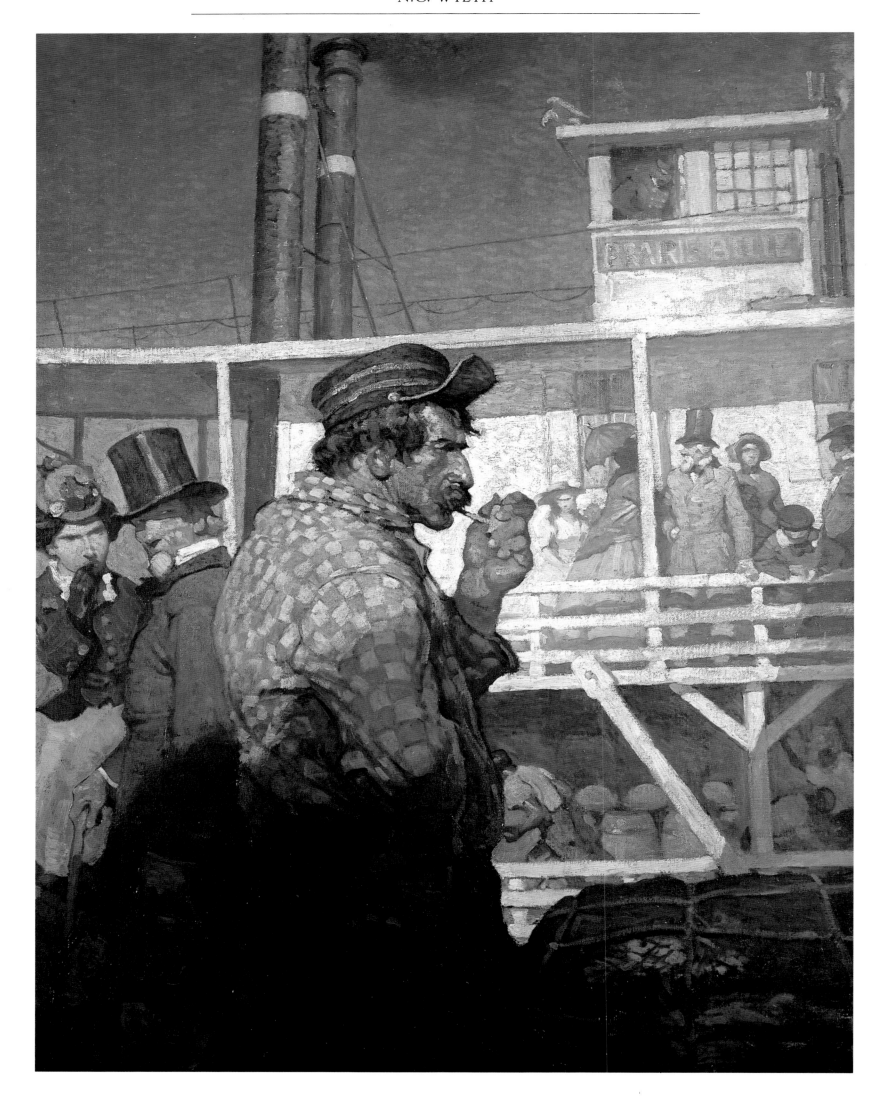

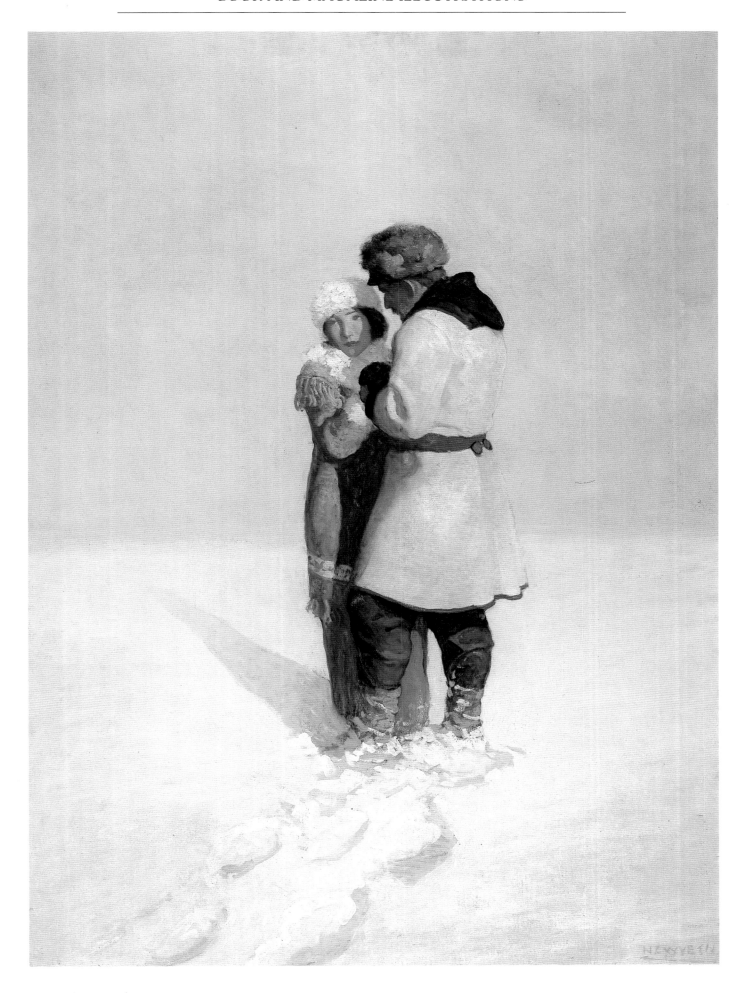

Left:
Jim Bludsoe, c. 1912
The Pike County Ballads by John Hay
Houghton Mifflin, Boston, 1912
Oil on canvas, 32½ × 25½ in.
Collected by C. T. and Claire McLaughlin
Diamond M Foundation Fine Art Collection, Lubbock, TX
Photography by Nicky Olson

At last, however, she had let Pascal Sarotte see her mind, 1913
"The Great Minus" by Gilbert Parker
Scribner's Magazine, December 1913
Oil on canvas, 43½ × 31½ in.
Photograph courtesy of Brandywine Fantasy Gallery, Chicago, IL

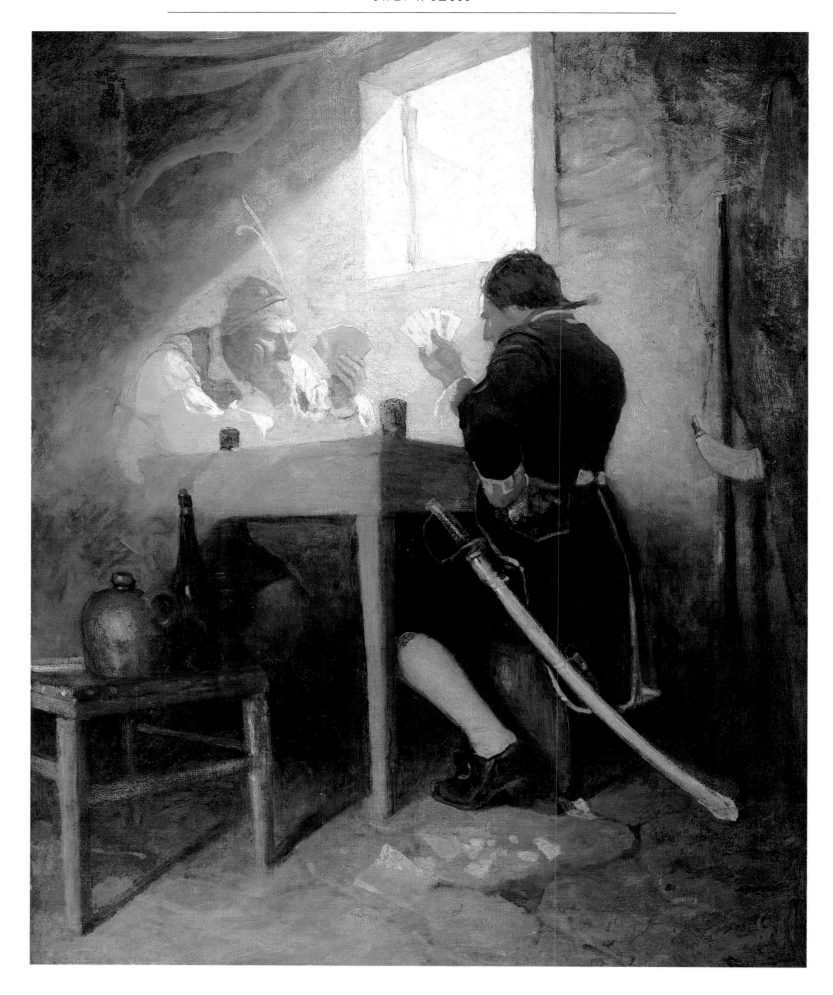

At the Cards in Cluny's Cage, 1913
Kidnapped by Robert Louis Stevenson
Charles Scribner's Sons, 1913
Oil on canvas, 40 × 32 in.
Bequest of Mrs. Russell G. Colt
Collection of the Brandywine River Museum, Chadds Ford, PA
Photography by Peter Ralston

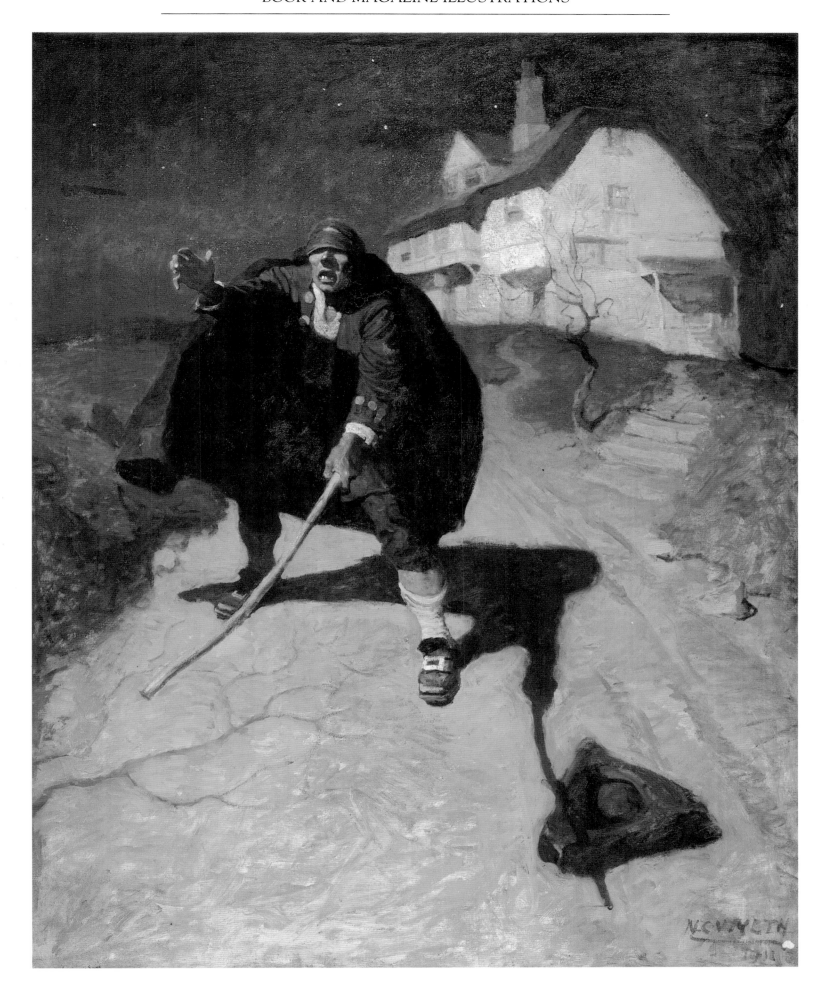

Old Pew (Blind Pew), 1911
Treasure Island by Robert Louis Stevenson
Charles Scribner's Sons, 1911
Oil on canvas, 47 × 38 in.
Collection of Mr. and Mrs. Andrew Wyeth
Photograph courtesy of the Brandywine River Museum
Photography by Peter Ralston

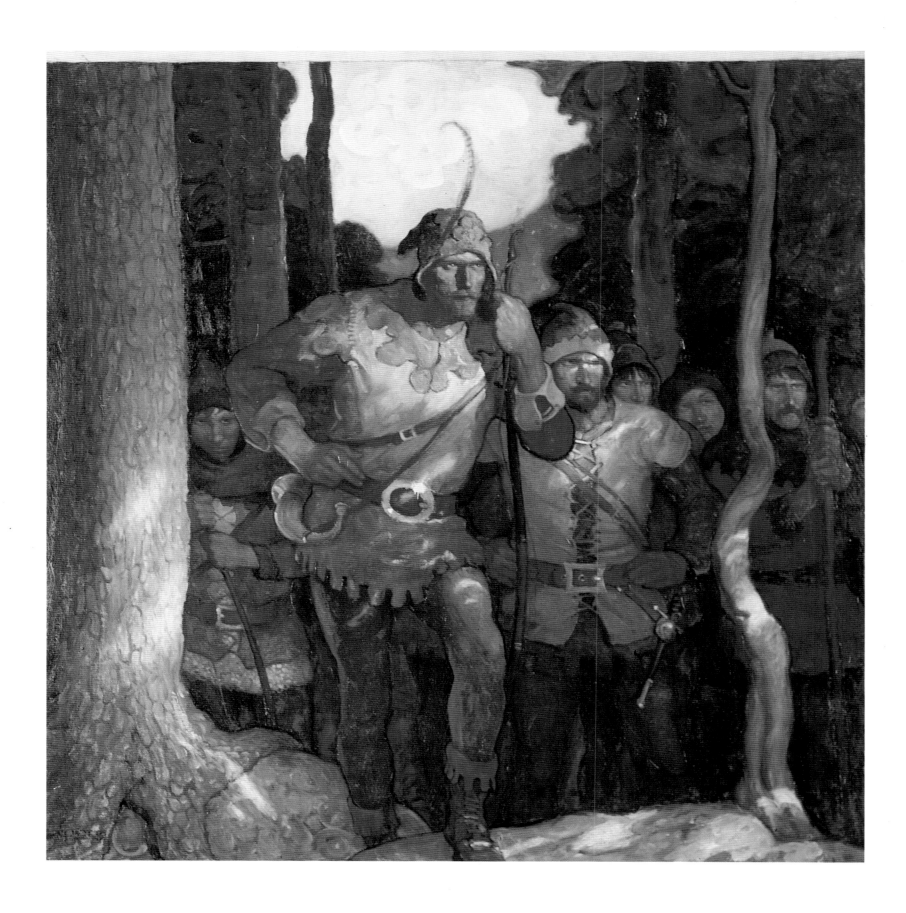

Robin Hood and the Men of Greenwood, 1917
Cover, *Robin Hood* by Paul Creswick
David McKay, Publishers, 1917
Oil on canvas
Collection of the New York Public Library, New York, NY
Photograph courtesy of the Brandywine River Museum
Photography by Peter Ralston

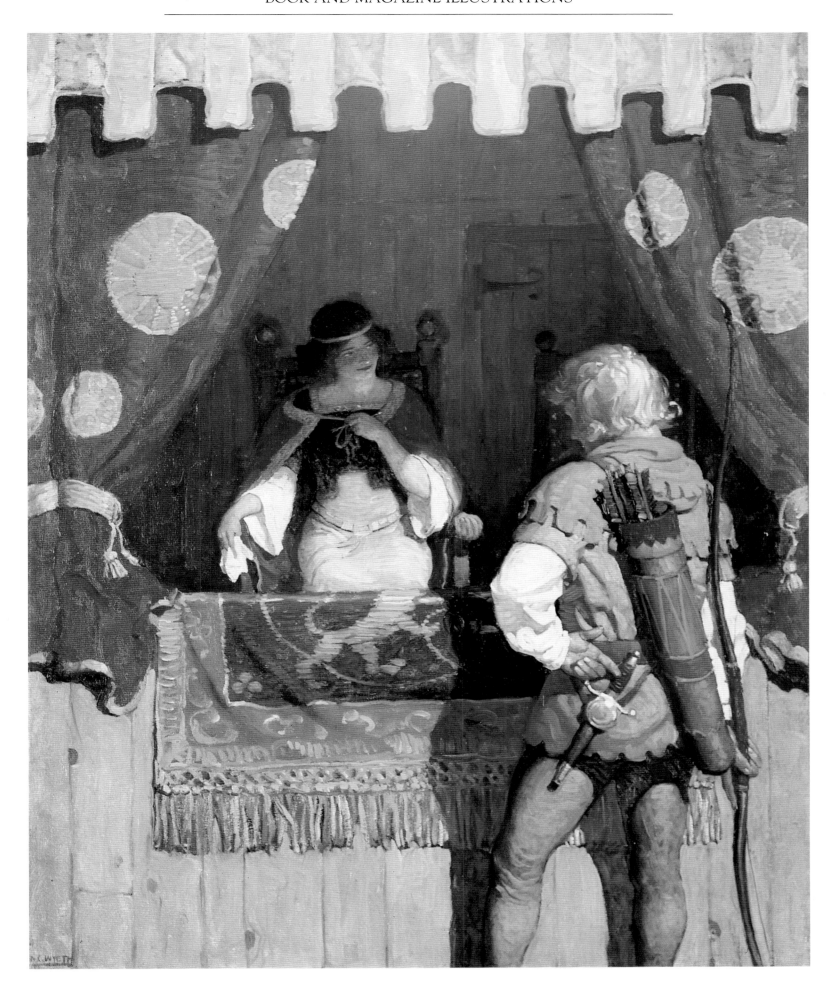

Robin Meets Maid Marion, 1917
Robin Hood by Paul Creswick
David McKay, Publishers, 1917
Oil on canvas
Collection of the New York Public Library, Central Children's Room,
Donnell Library Center, New York, NY
Photograph courtesy of the Brandywine River Museum
Photography by Peter Ralston

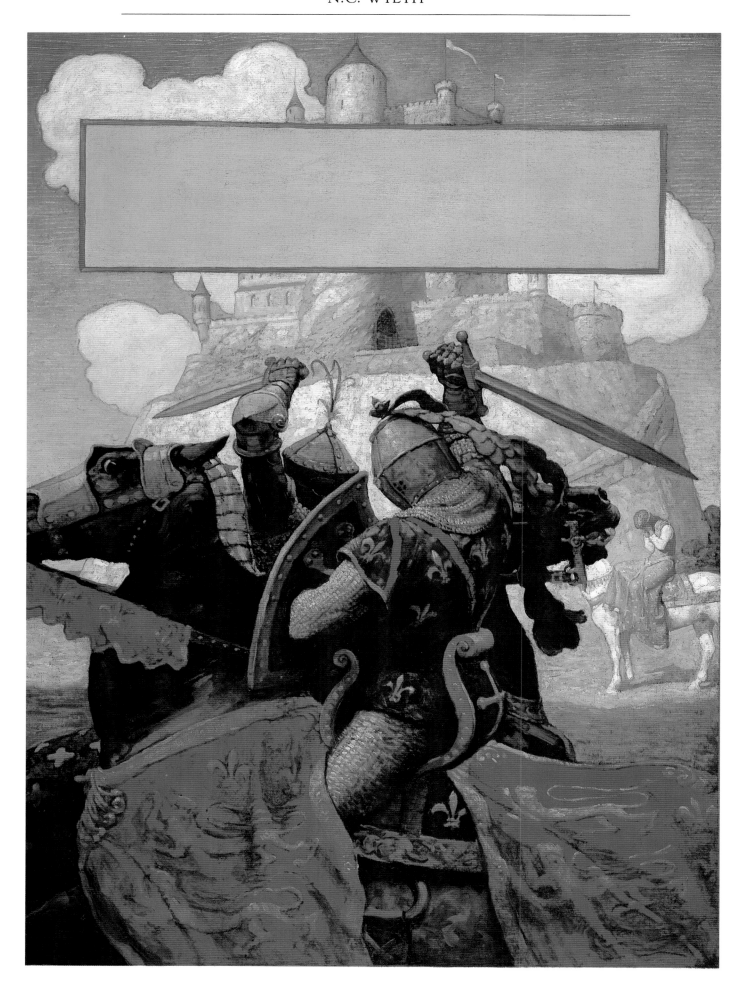

The Boy's King Arthur, 1917
Cover, *The Boy's King Arthur* edited by Sidney Lanier
Charles Scribner's Sons, 1917
Oil on canvas, 40⅝ × 29⅞ in.
Courtesy of Caroline and John Grayson Milne
Photography by Peter Ralston

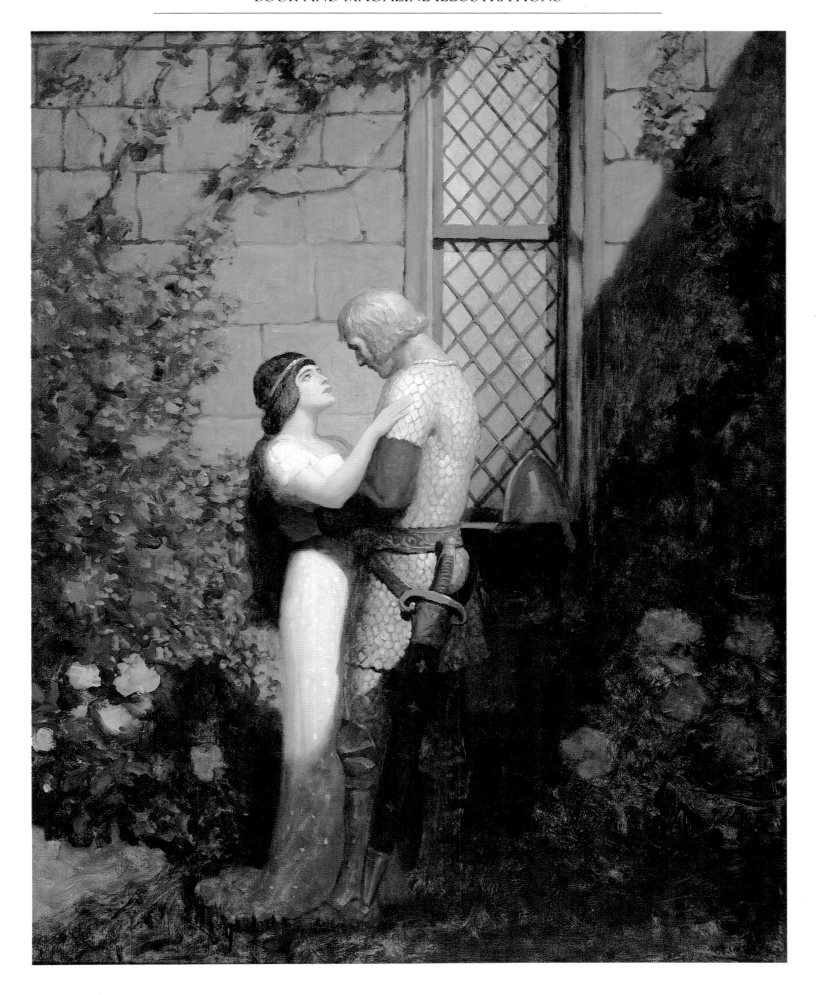

Sir Tristram and La Belle Isolde in the Garden, 1917
The Boy's King Arthur edited by Sidney Lanier
Charles Scribner's Sons, 1917
Oil on canvas, 39¾ × 32 in.
Collection of the Brandywine River Museum, Chadds Ford, PA
Photography by Peter Ralston

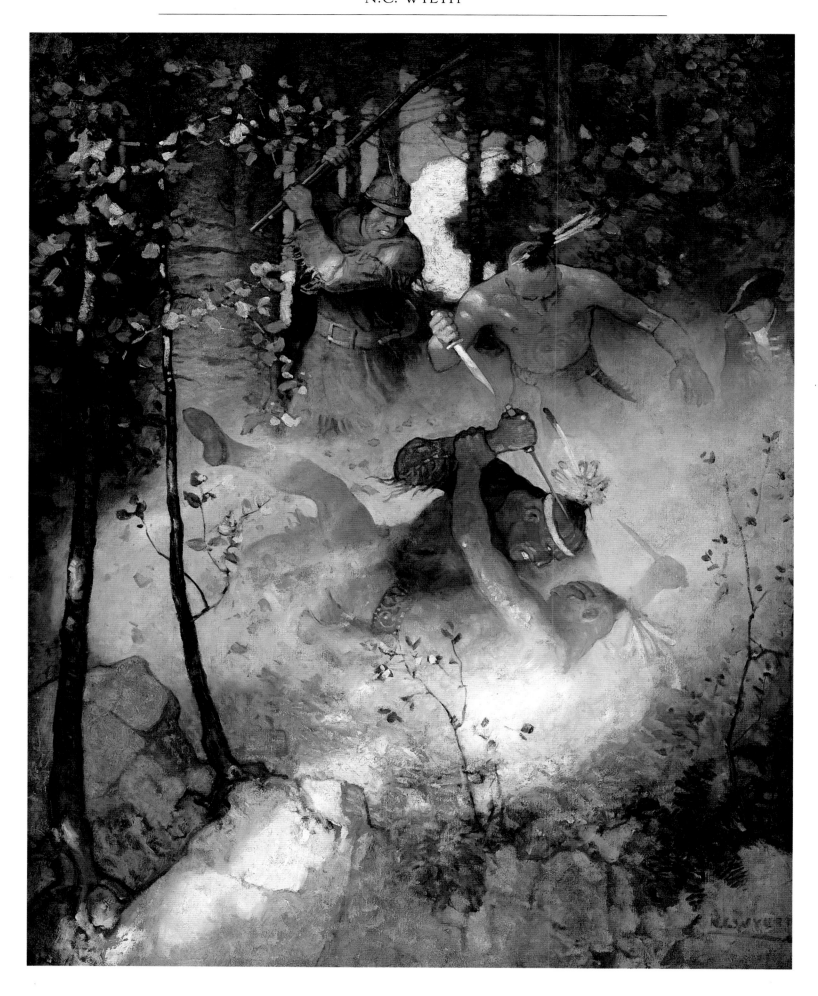

The Fight in the Forest, c. 1918
The Last of the Mohicans by James Fenimore Cooper
Charles Scribner's Sons, 1919
Oil on canvas, 40½ × 32¼ in.
Collection of the Brandywine River Museum, Chadds Ford, PA
Photography by Peter Ralston

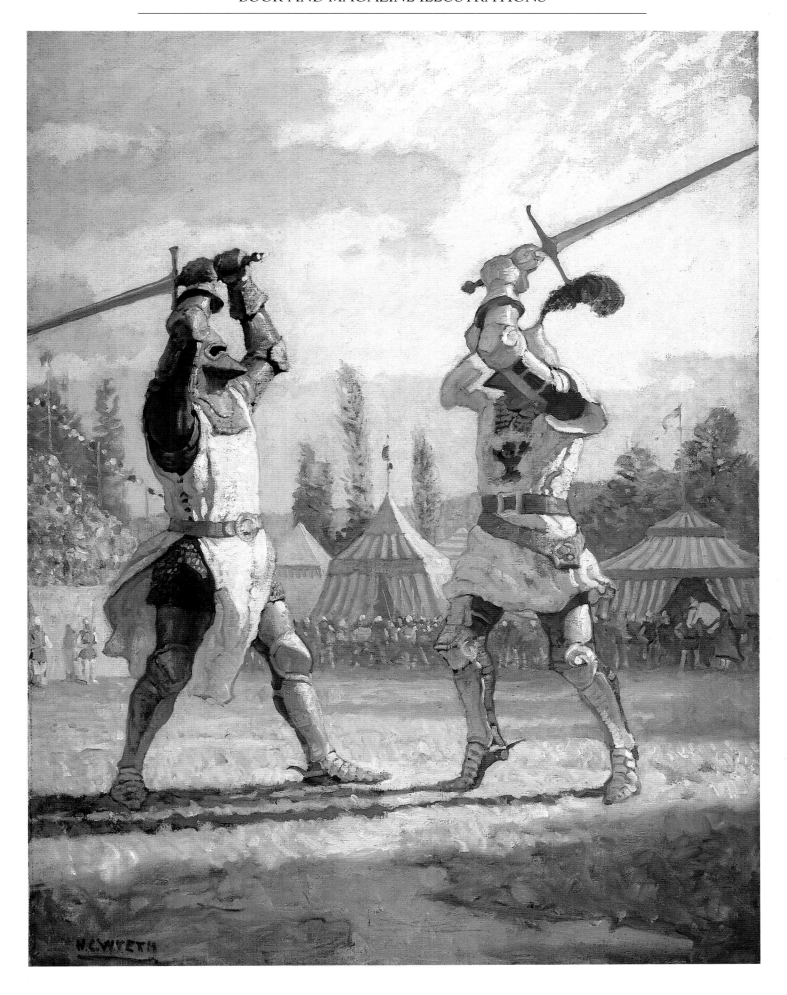

Sir Nigel Sustains England's Honor in the Lists, 1922
The White Company by Sir Arthur Conan Doyle
Cosmopolitan Book Corporation, 1922
Oil on canvas, 40 × 30¼ in.
Courtesy of Millport Conservancy
Photography by Peter Ralston

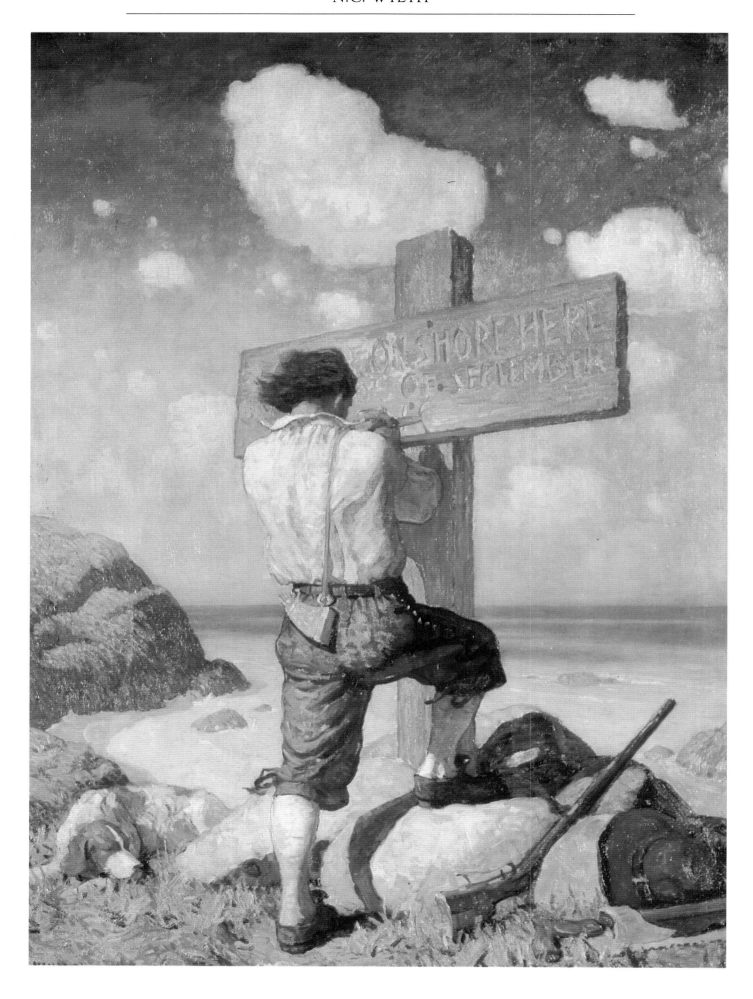

**"– and making it into a great cross,
I set it up on the shore where I first landed – ,"** 1920
Robinson Crusoe by Daniel Defoe
Cosmopolitan Book Corporation
Oil on canvas
Collection of the Wilmington Institute Library, DE
Photograph courtesy of the Brandywine River Museum
Photography by Peter Ralston

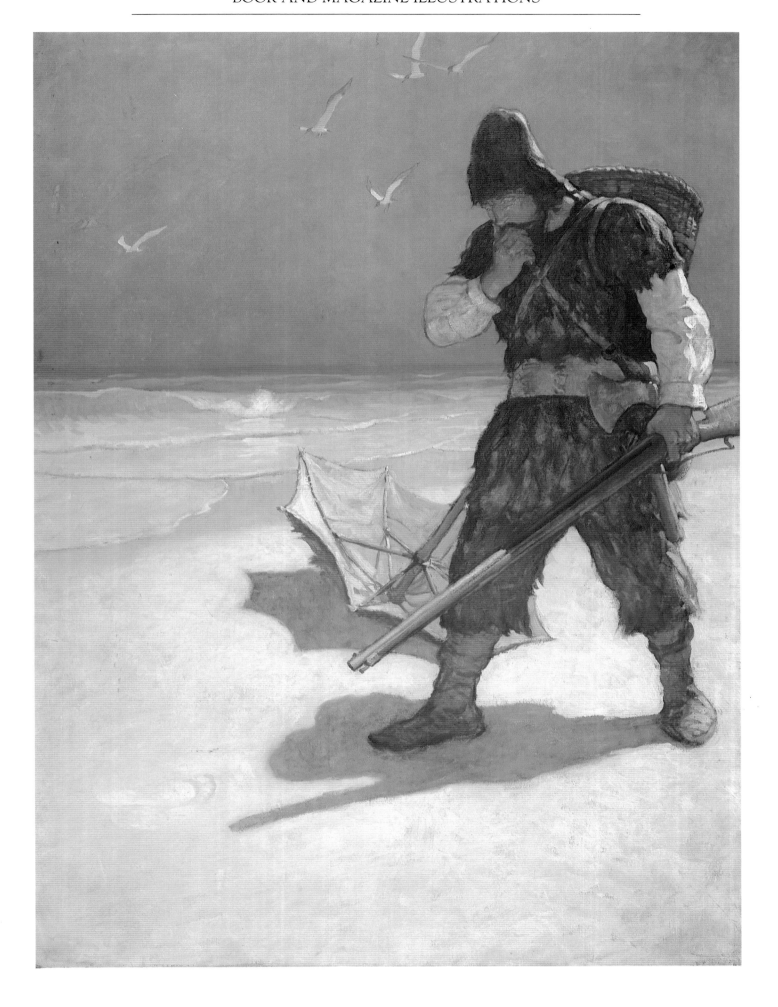

"I stood like one thunderstruck or as if I had seen an apparition," 1920
Robinson Crusoe by Daniel Defoe
Cosmopolitan Book Corporation
Oil on canvas, 40 × 30 in.
Collection of the Wilmington Institute Library, DE
Photograph courtesy of the Brandywine River Museum
Photography by Peter Ralston

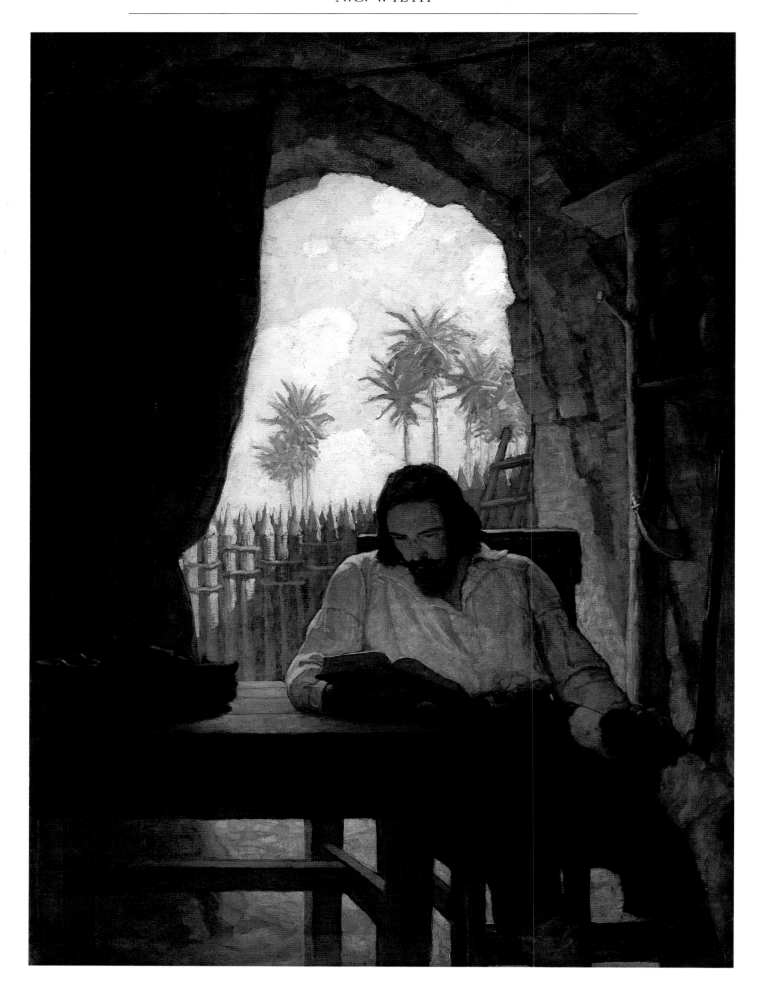

**And in the morning I took the Bible; and beginning at
the New Testament I began seriously to read it,** 1920
Robinson Crusoe by Daniel Defoe
Cosmopolitan Book Corporation
Oil on canvas
Collection of the Wilmington Institute Library, DE
Photography by Peter Ralston

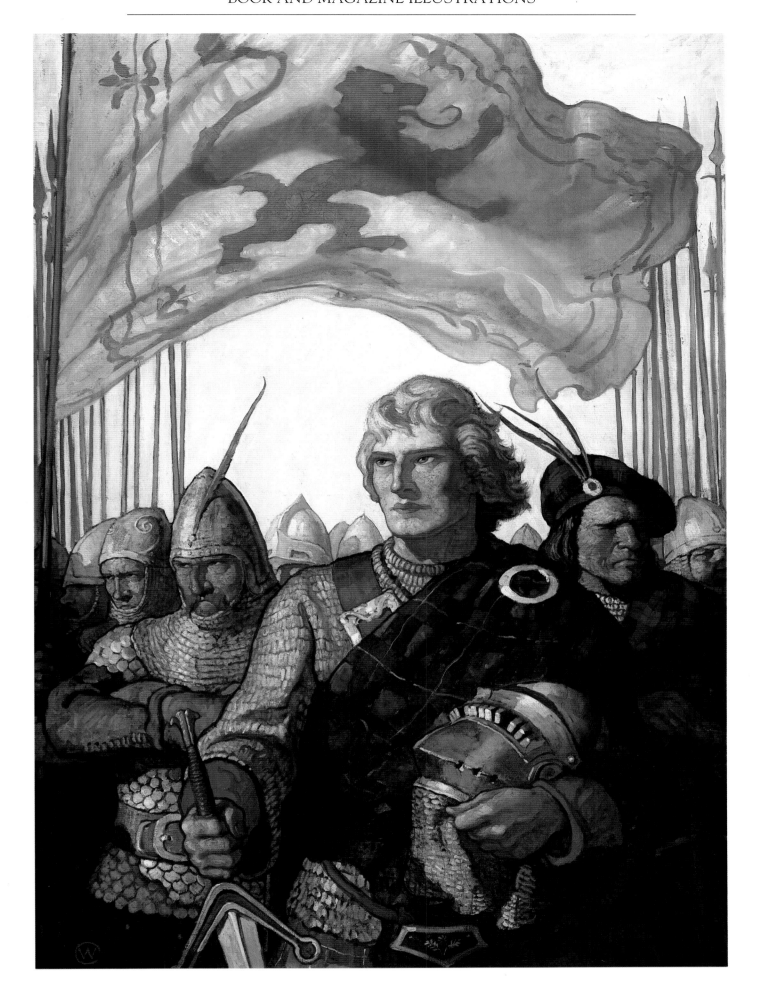

Scottish Chiefs, 1921
Cover, *Scottish Chiefs* by Jane Porter
Charles Scribner's Sons, 1921
Oil on canvas
Permanent Collection of the University of Delaware, Wilmington, DE
Photography by Peter Ralston

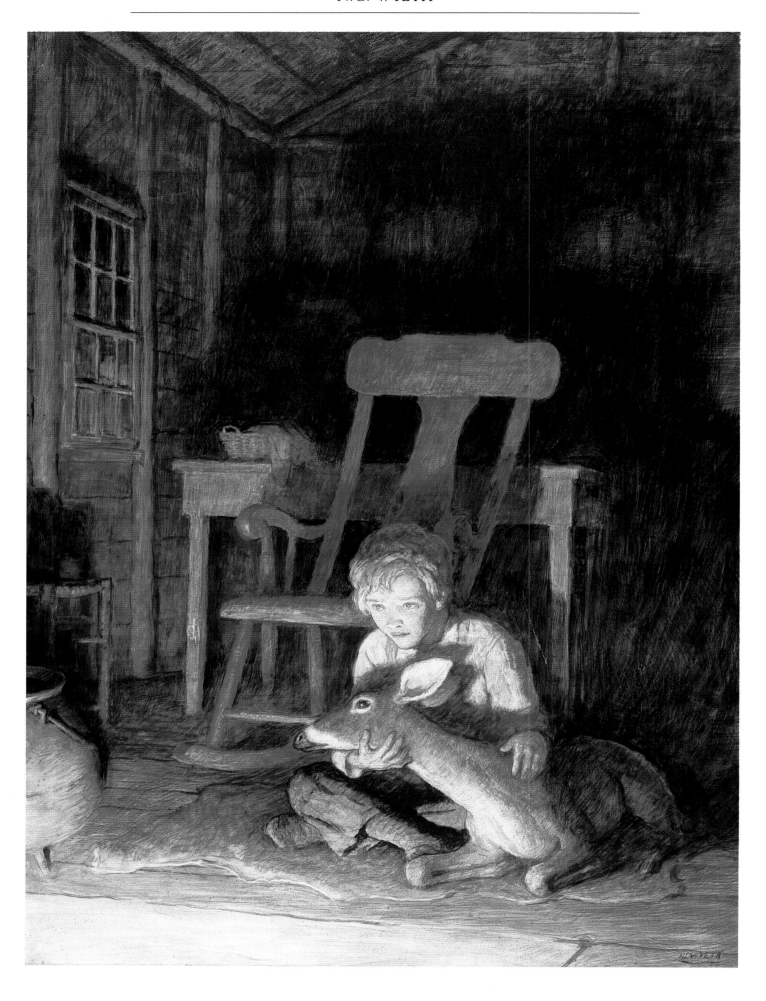

Jody and Flag, 1939
The Yearling by Marjorie Kinnan Rawlings
Charles Scribner's Sons, 1939
Oil on canvas, 45 × 32 in.
Private Collection
Photography by Peter Ralston

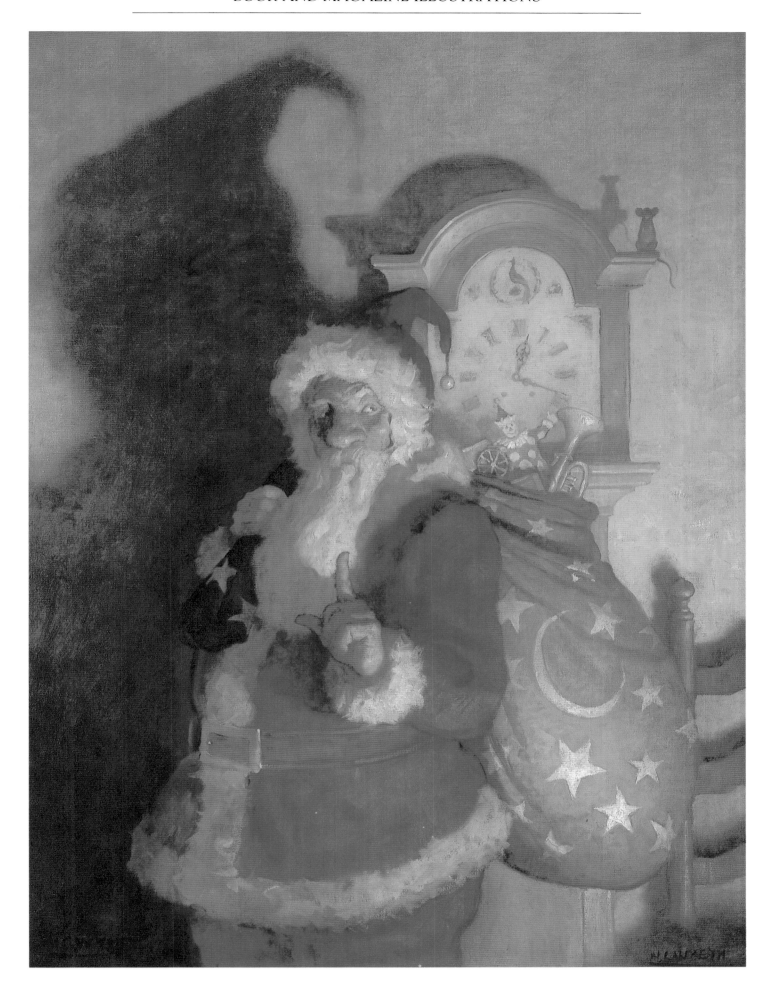

Old Kris, 1925
Cover, *Country Gentleman,* December 1925
Oil on canvas, 34 × 30½ in.
© 1985 by A. B. McCoy
Photograph courtesy of the Brandywine River Museum

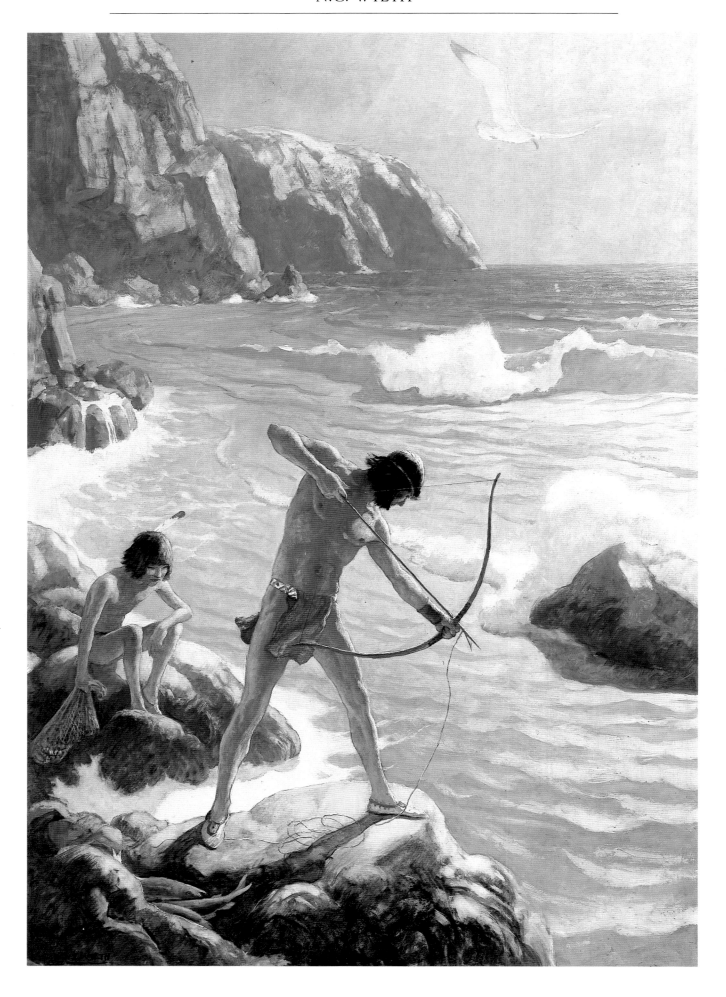

The First Maine Fisherman, 1937
Trending Into Maine by Kenneth Roberts
Little, Brown and Company, 1938
Oil on panel, 35 × 25 in.
Photograph courtesy of the Brandywine Fantasy Gallery, Chicago, IL

Right:
She Makes a Grand Light (The Burning of the *Bounty*), 1940
The Bounty Trilogy by Charles Nordoff and James Norman Hall
Little, Brown and Company
Oil on canvas, 34 × 25 in.
Courtesy of the Free Library of Philadelphia, PA
Photography by Nate Clark

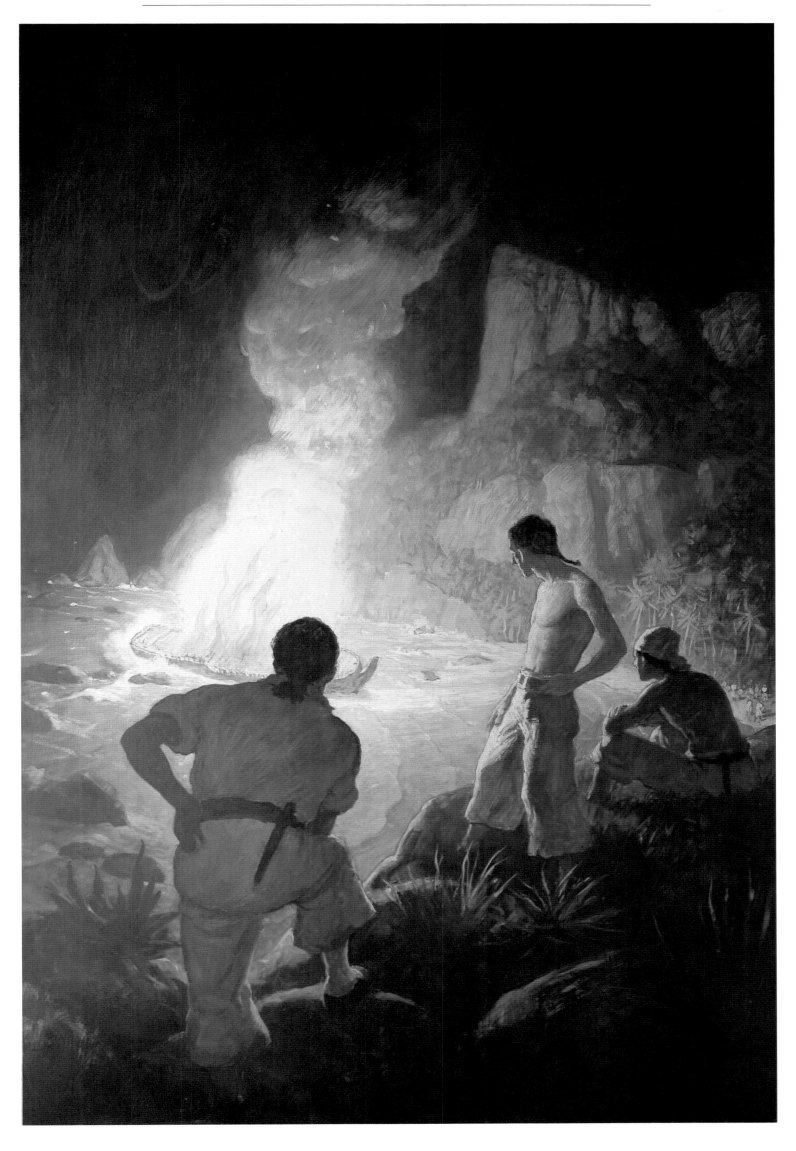

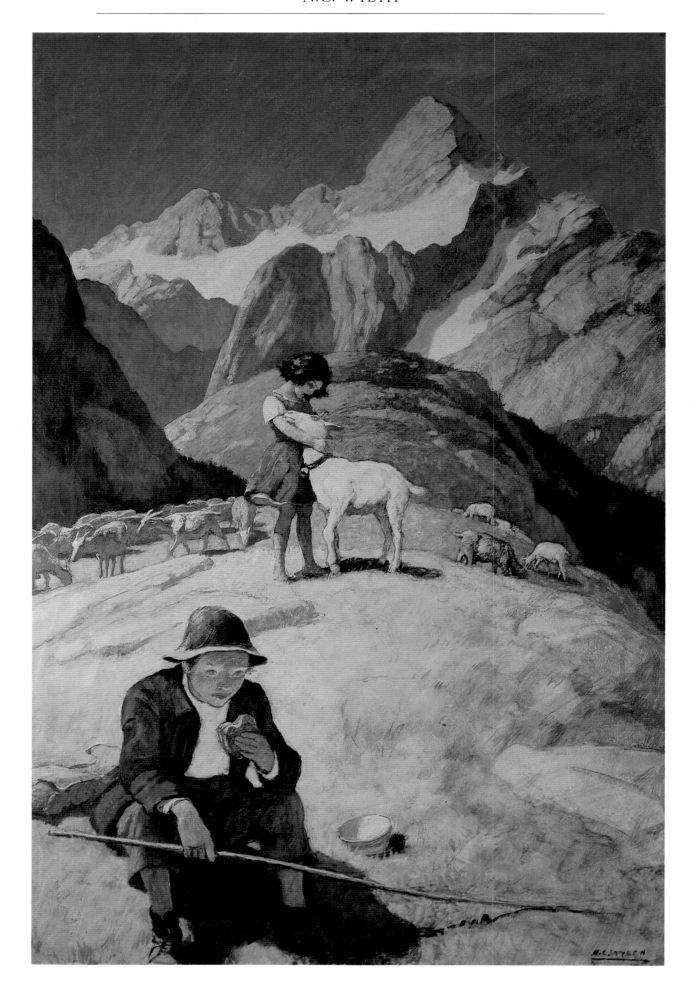

Heidi, 1940
Anthology of Children's Literature compiled by
Edna Johnson and Carrie E. Scott
Houghton Mifflin Company, 1940
Oil on canvas
Courtesy of the Free Library of Philadelphia, PA

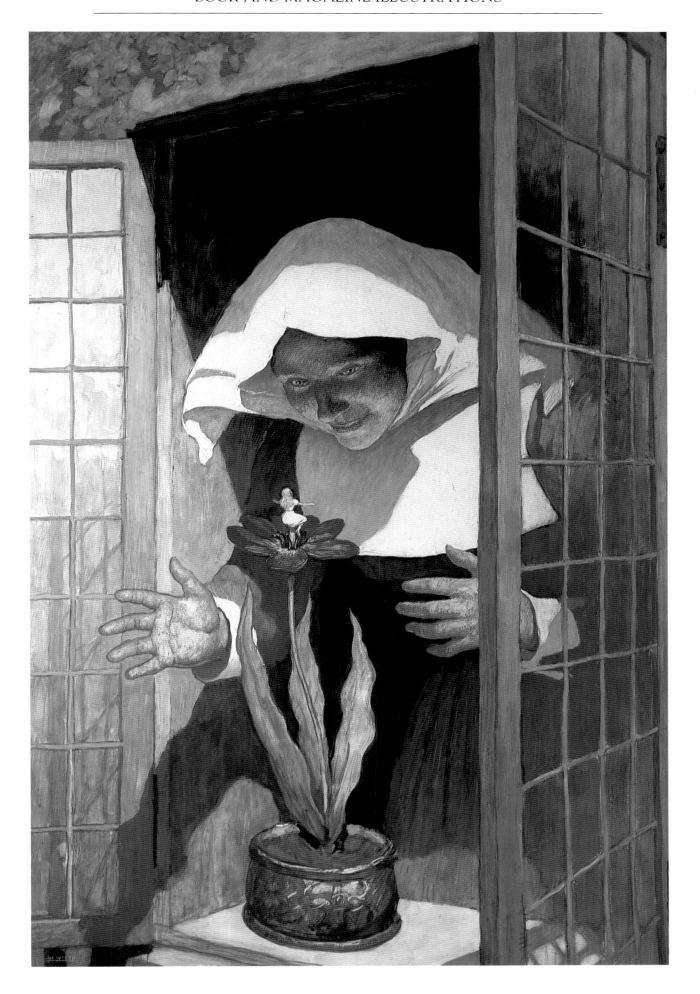

Thumbelisa, 1940
Anthology of Children's Literature compiled by
Edna Johnson and Carrie E. Scott
Houghton Mifflin Company, 1940
Oil on canvas
Courtesy of the Free Library of Philadelphia, PA

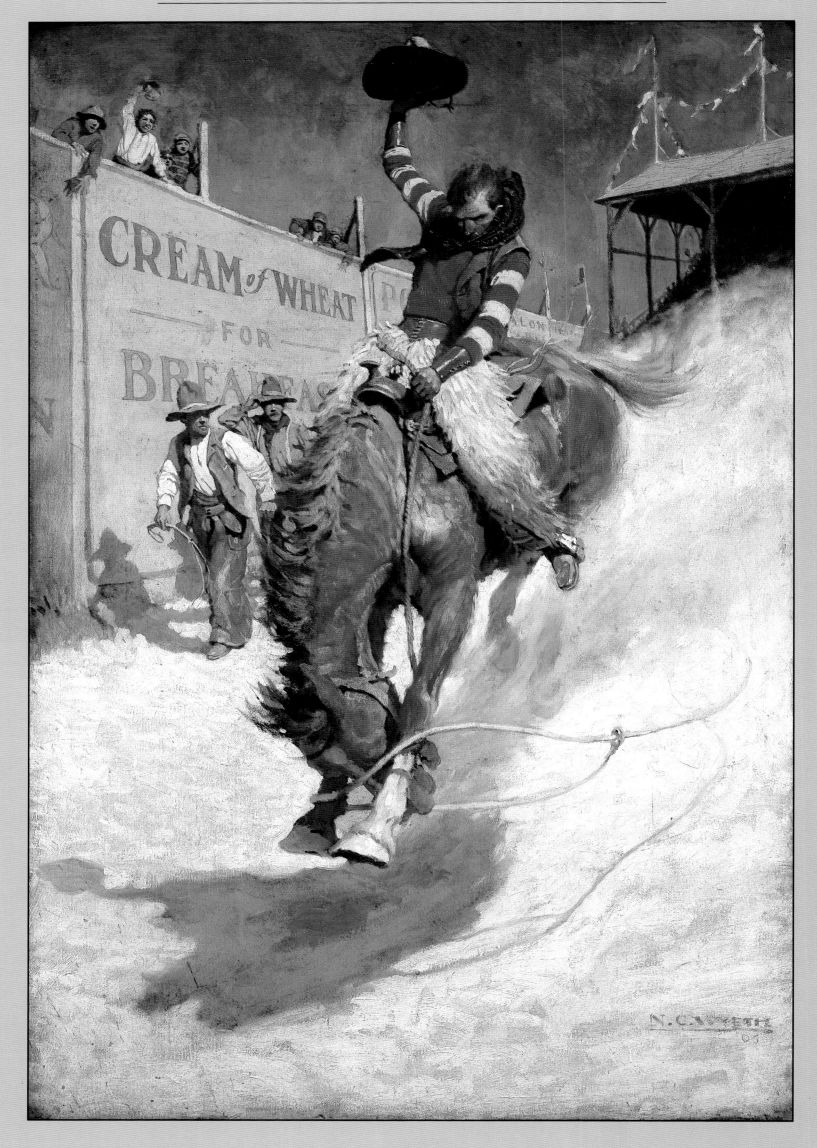

COMMERCIAL ILLUSTRATIONS, CALENDARS, AND MURALS

N.C. Wyeth's extraordinary illustrative talent was particularly well-suited for commercial assignments such as print advertising, calendars, and public murals. Early on he did canvases for the Cream of Wheat cereal company featuring cowboys out on the prairies and sled dogs in Alaska. He had a variety of clients including the Coca-Cola Company, the Pennsylvania Railroad, the General Electric Company, and Joseph E. Seagram & Sons. The company may have determined the subject on occasion but he chose his own color schemes and pictorial composition.

State universities and several financial institutions offered Wyeth lucrative commissions for large scale murals of historic battles and renowned figures to decorate their walls and offices. The great size of these murals did not daunt N.C. Wyeth. He was a large man with tremendous physical stamina and when necessary he would work night and day to paint his canvases on location.

For Fisk Tires, Wyeth painted a tropical scene of native workers bearing rubber to a waiting steamer. For the Quaker Oats Company, he portrayed Aunt Jemima at the 1893 World's Fair to advertise their pancake mix.

Wyeth did illustrations for calendars, too, printed for firms like the John Morell Co., focusing on American history. A fine painting of a broncobuster touts Cream of Wheat cereal on a background billboard.

Hoteliers were also customers of Wyeth's murals. Working on a project with the famous architect William Price, who designed the Pennsylvania Terminal in New York and Union Station in Chicago, Wyeth painted mermaids and sea dragons for the underground café at the Hotel Traymore in Atlantic City, New Jersey. Where some of his customers may have desired traditional themes, here the emphasis was on a modern look.

For the Hotel Utica in Utica, New York, the artist provided the design for their china that shows an Indian paddling a canoe quietly on a serene waterway. Frederic Remington and Maxfield Parrish were also employed on projects at the Hotel Utica, and Wyeth was proud to work in tandem with them.

For the Federal Reserve Bank in Boston, N.C. Wyeth painted two 10- by 13-foot panels, one of Alexander Hamilton and George Washington and the second of Abraham Lincoln and Salmon Chase.

N.C. Wyeth's paintings for the state capitol building in St. Louis, Missouri, were historic scenes of Wilson's Creek Battle and the Battle of Westport – panoramic vistas of horses and cavalrymen. His poster design for the U.S. Naval Department in 1917 was a large canvas of Neptune, the Roman sea god, bearing his triton aloft to protect the American ships and sailors during the course of World War I. Two of Carolyn Wyeth's brothers were involved with the American naval effort and Wyeth was proud to contribute his share to the government.

Some of the last murals Wyeth painted were a series for the Metropolitan Life Insurance Company in New York. One of these, of egrets gliding effortlessly along in the skies above a river, is a romantic, ethereal composition. Although he was killed in a train accident before the murals' completion, his son Andrew and another one of his art pupils carried on for him.

Bronco Buster, 1907
Advertisement, Cream of Wheat
Oil on canvas
Gift of the National Biscuit Company
Courtesy of the Minneapolis Institute of Arts, Minneapolis, MN

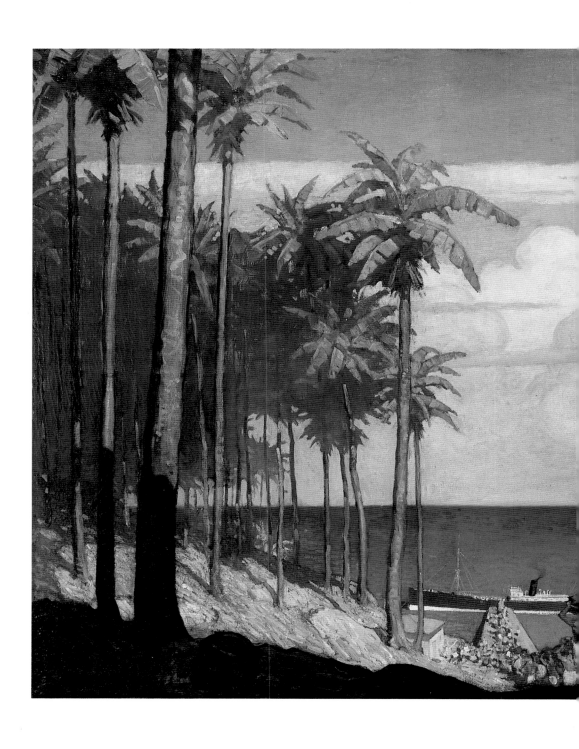

From the Forests of Ceylon, 1917
Advertisement, Fisk Cord Tire Company, 1918
Oil on canvas, 31 × 67 in.
Photograph courtesy of Brandywine Fantasy Gallery, Chicago, IL

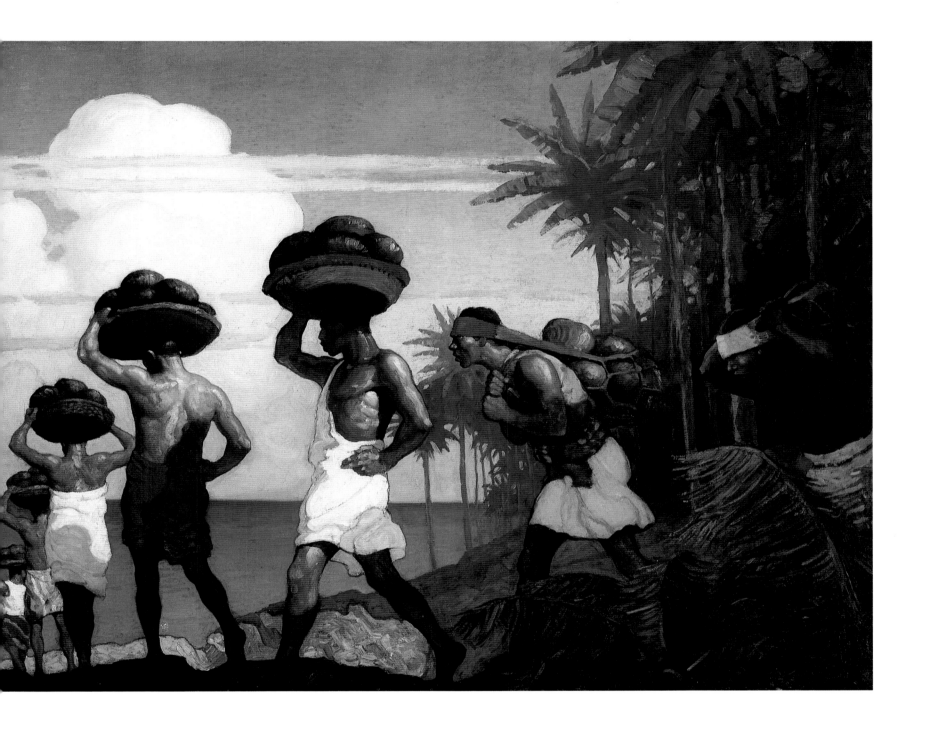

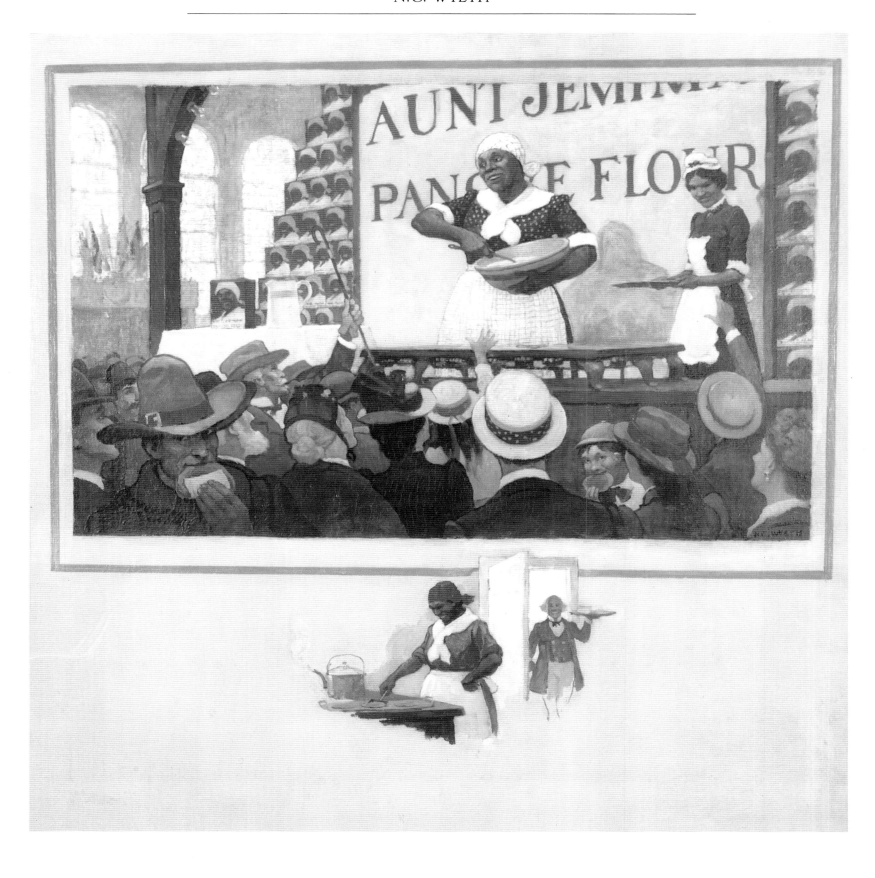

Aunt Jemima at the Columbian Exposition in 1893, c. 1919
Advertisement, Aunt Jemima Mills Company, 1921
Courtesy of the Quaker Oats Company, St. Joseph, MO

Right:
Coca-Cola Calendar Illustration, 1937
Courtesy of the Coca-Cola Company Archives, Atlanta, GA

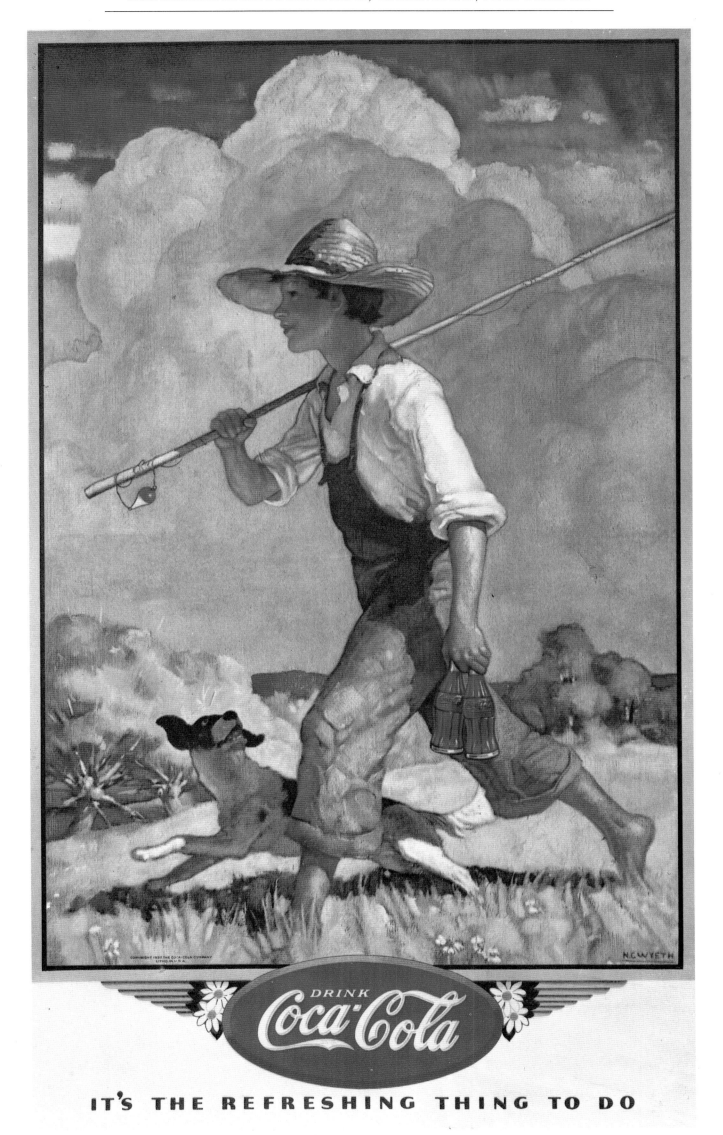

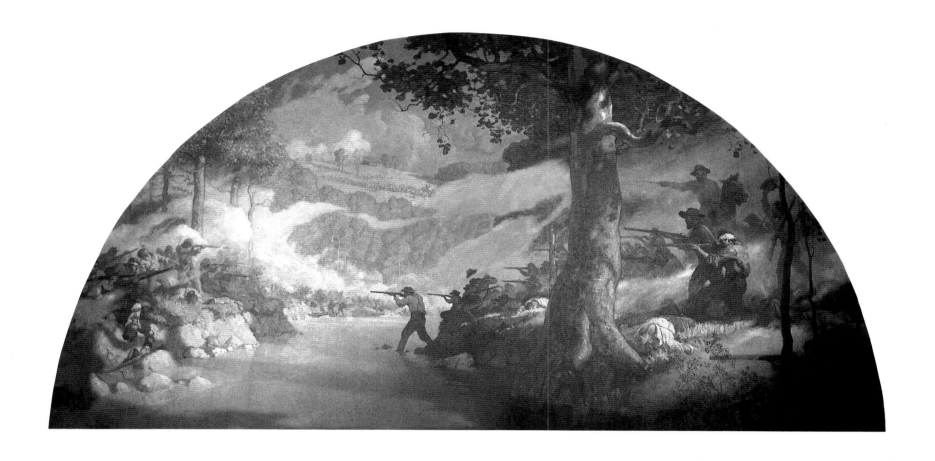

The Battle of Wilson's Creek, 1920
Oil on canvas, 72 × 144 in.
Courtesy of Missouri Department of Natural Resources,
Jefferson City, MO
Photography by Nick Decker

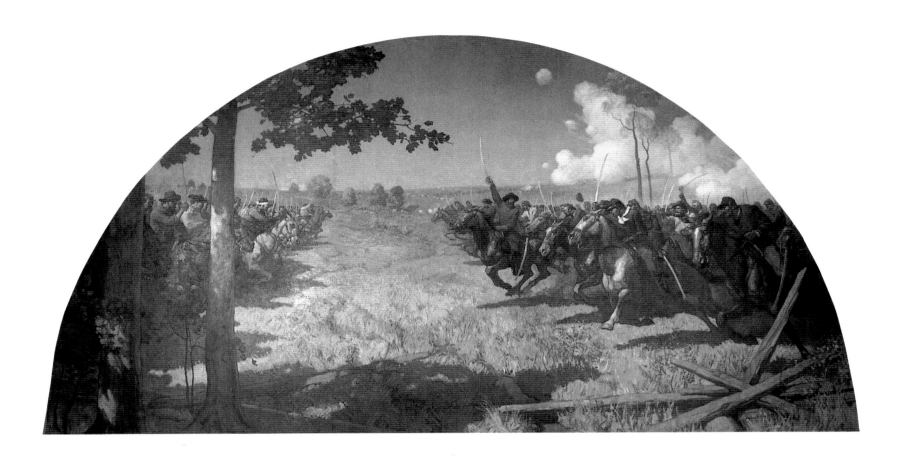

The Battle of Westport, 1920
Oil on canvas, 72 × 144 in.
Courtesy of Missouri Department of Natural Resources,
Jefferson City, MO
Photography by Nick Decker

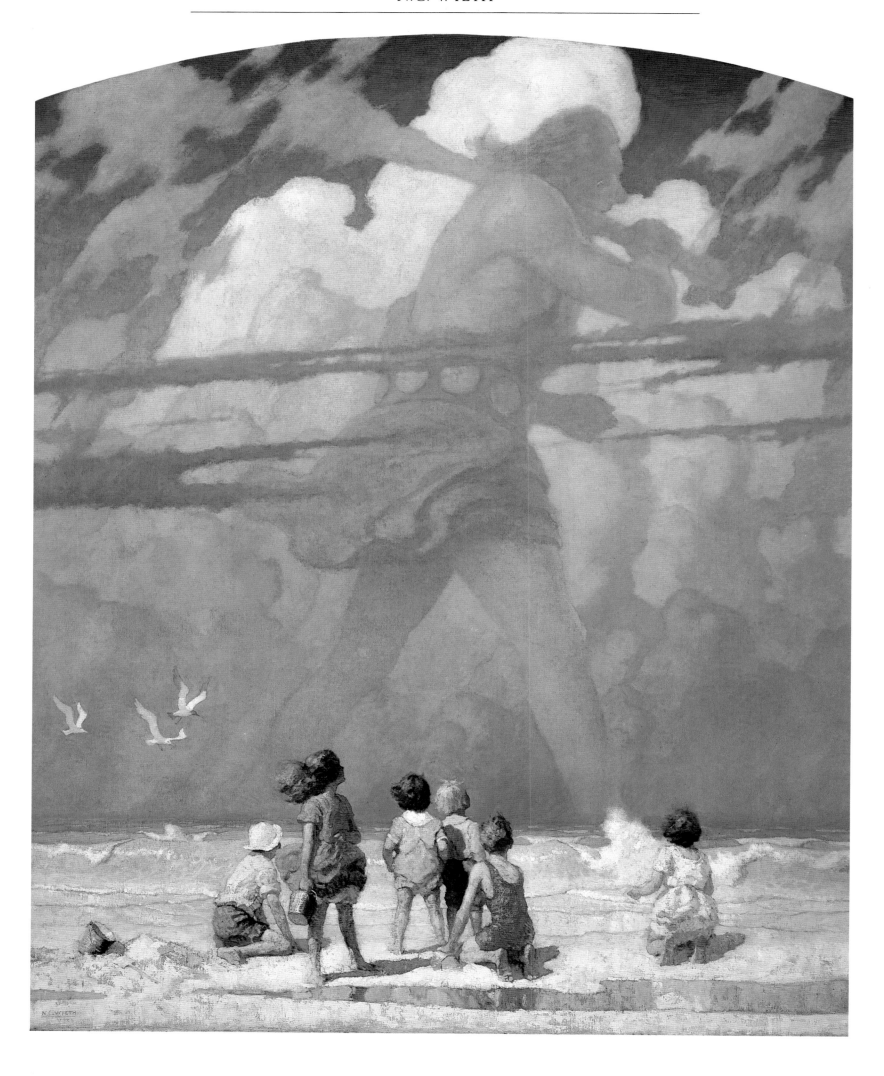

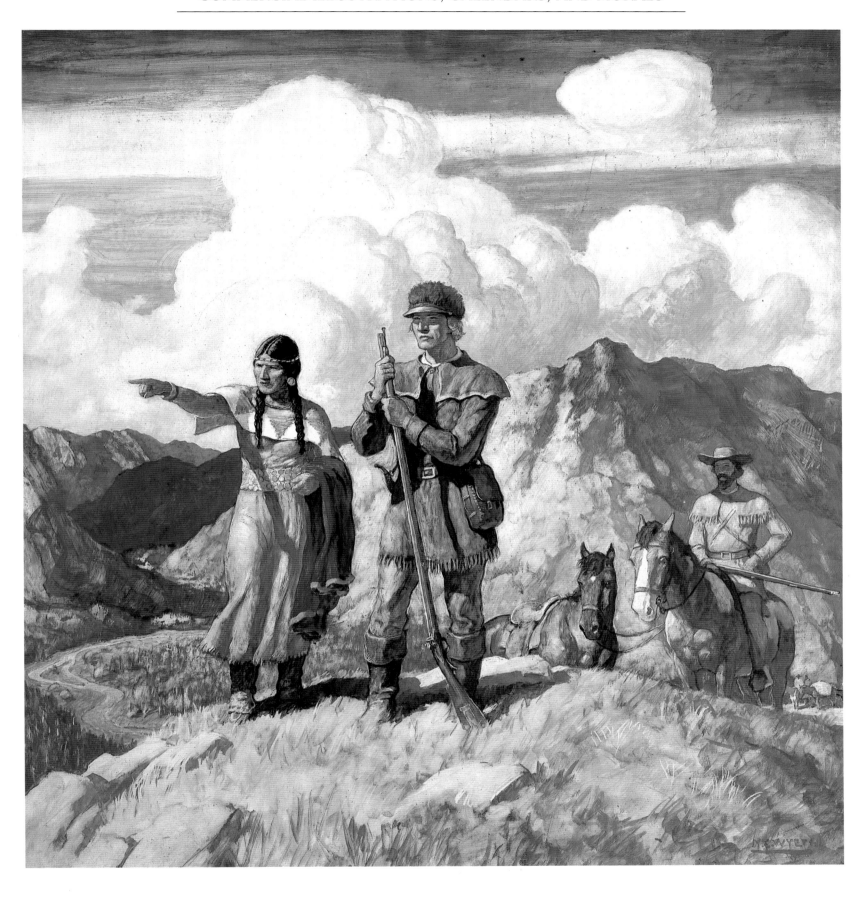

The Giant, 1923
Oil on canvas, 72 × 60 in.
Courtesy of the Westtown School, Westtown, PA
Photograph courtesy of the Brandywine River Museum

Lewis and Clark, 1939
America in the Making, Calendar published for
John Morrell & Company, Ottumwa, IA, 1940
Oil with some tempera on panel, 26½ × 24½ in.
Gift of John Morrell & Company, 1940
From the University Art Collection, Iowa State University, Ames, IA

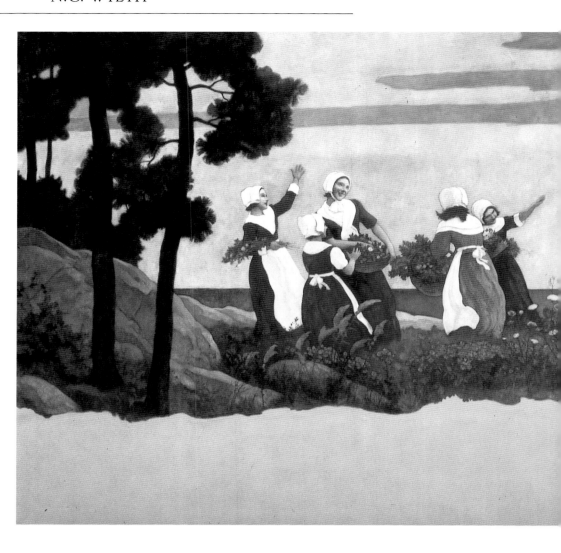

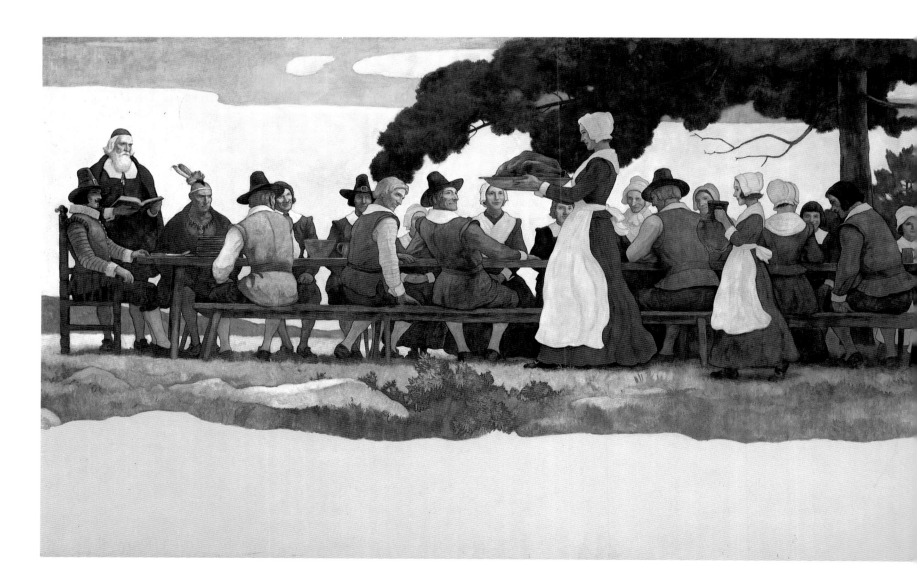

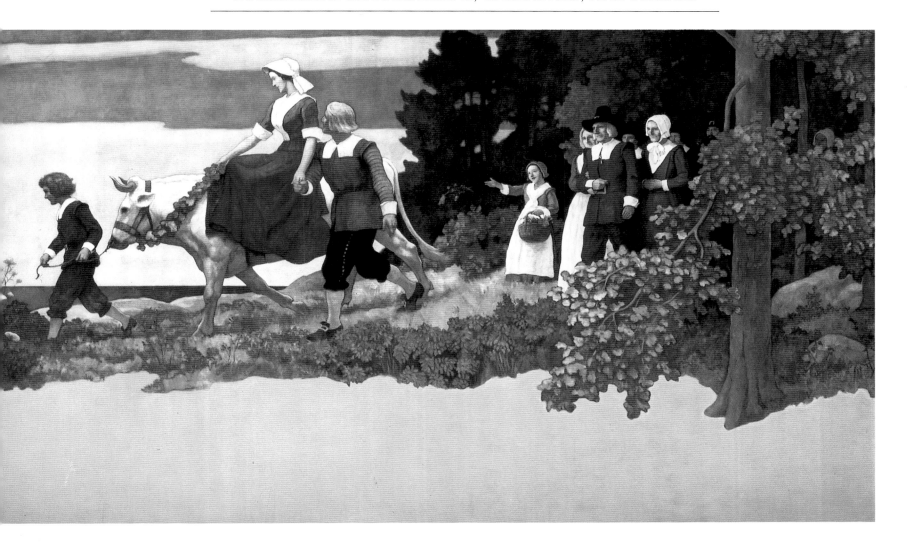

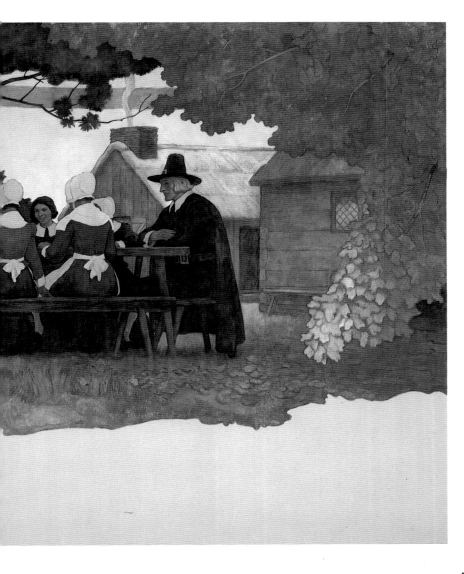

Top:
The Wedding Procession, 1940-1945
Oil on canvas, 108 × 300 in.
From the collection of the Metropolitan Life Insurance Company,
New York, NY
Photography by Malcolm Varon

Bottom:
The Thanksgiving Feast, 1940-1945
Oil on canvas, 108 × 284 in.
From the collection of the Metropolitan Life Insurance Company,
New York, NY
Photography by Malcolm Varon

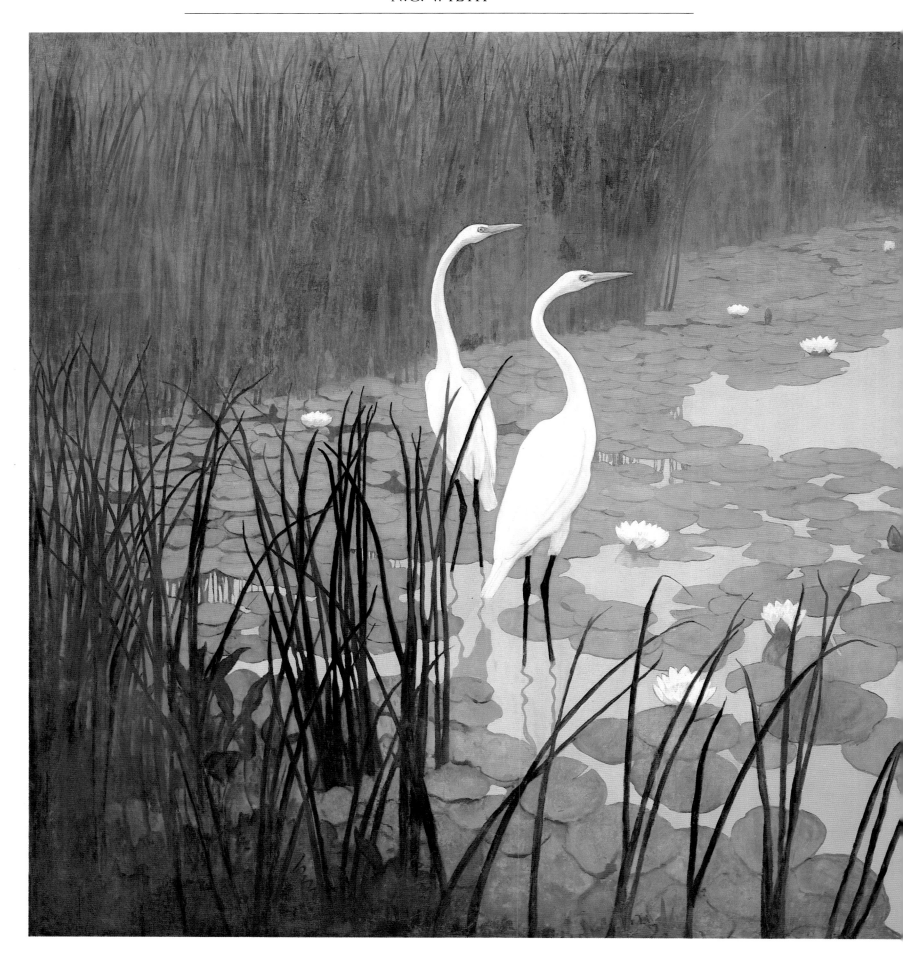

Egrets in Summer, 1940-1945
Oil on canvas, 82⅞ × 159 in.
From the collection of the Metropolitan Life Insurance Company,
New York, NY
Photography by Malcolm Varon

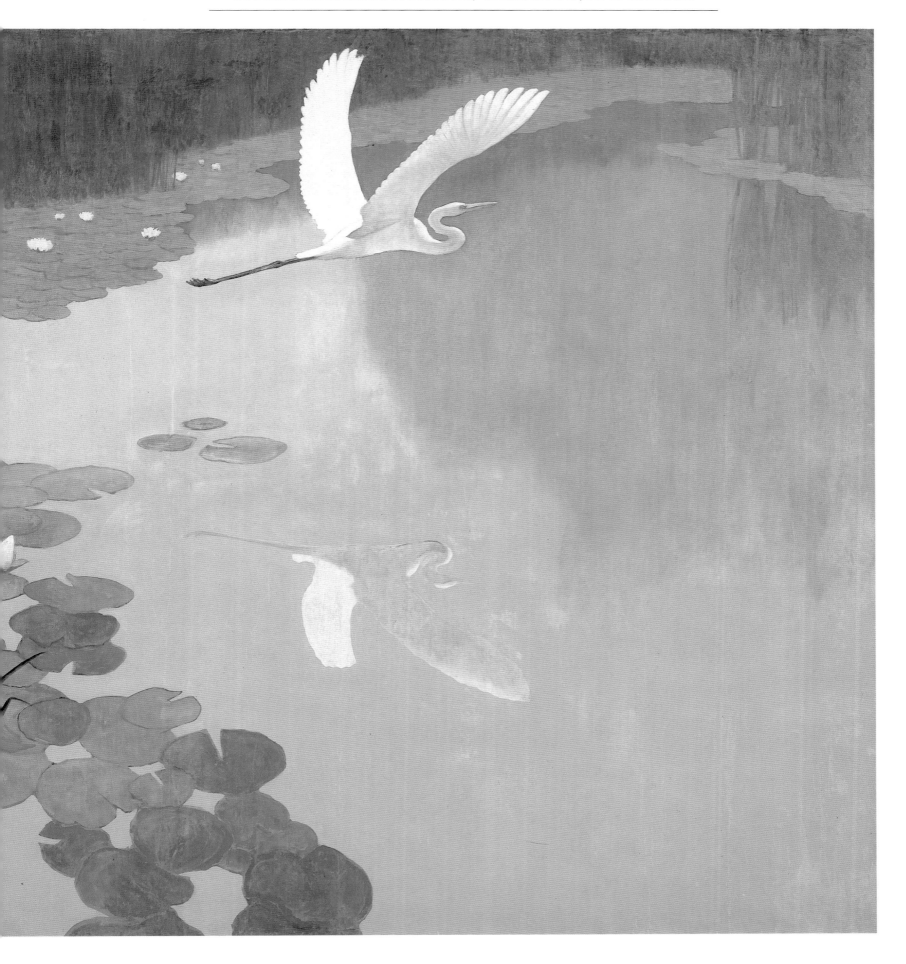

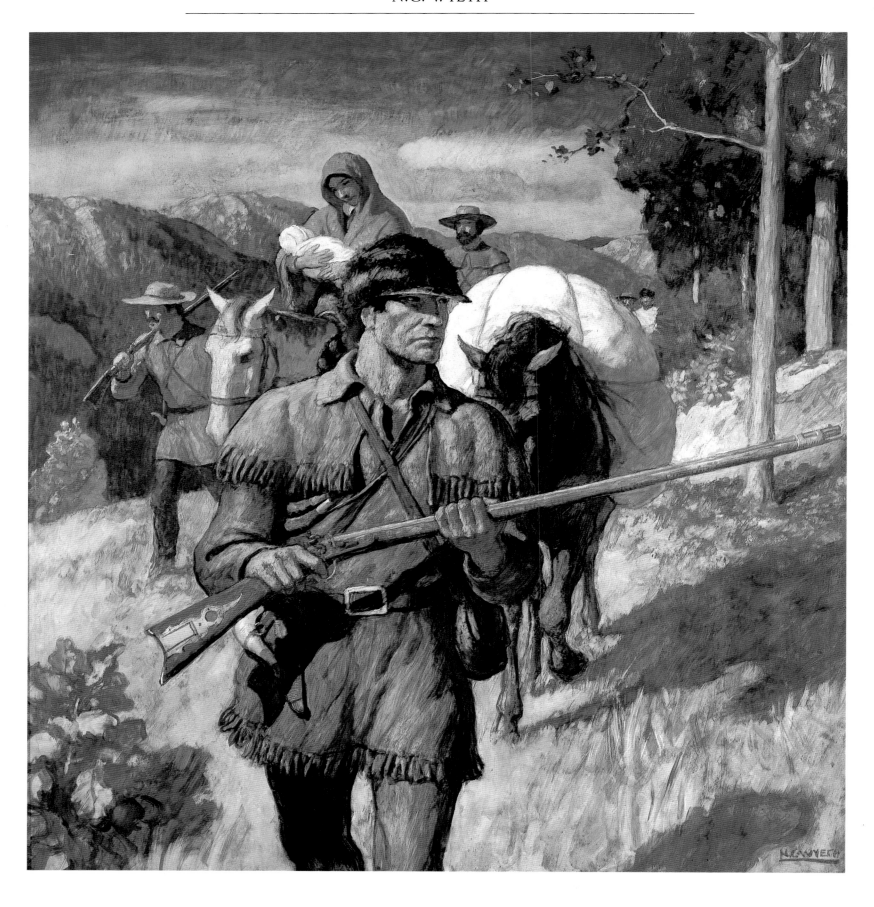

Daniel Boone, 1940
America in the Making, Calendar published for
John Morrell & Company, Ottumwa, IA, 1940
Oil with some areas of tempera on panel, 26¾ × 25 in.
Gift of John Morrell & Company, 1940
From the University Art Collection, Iowa State University, Ames, IA

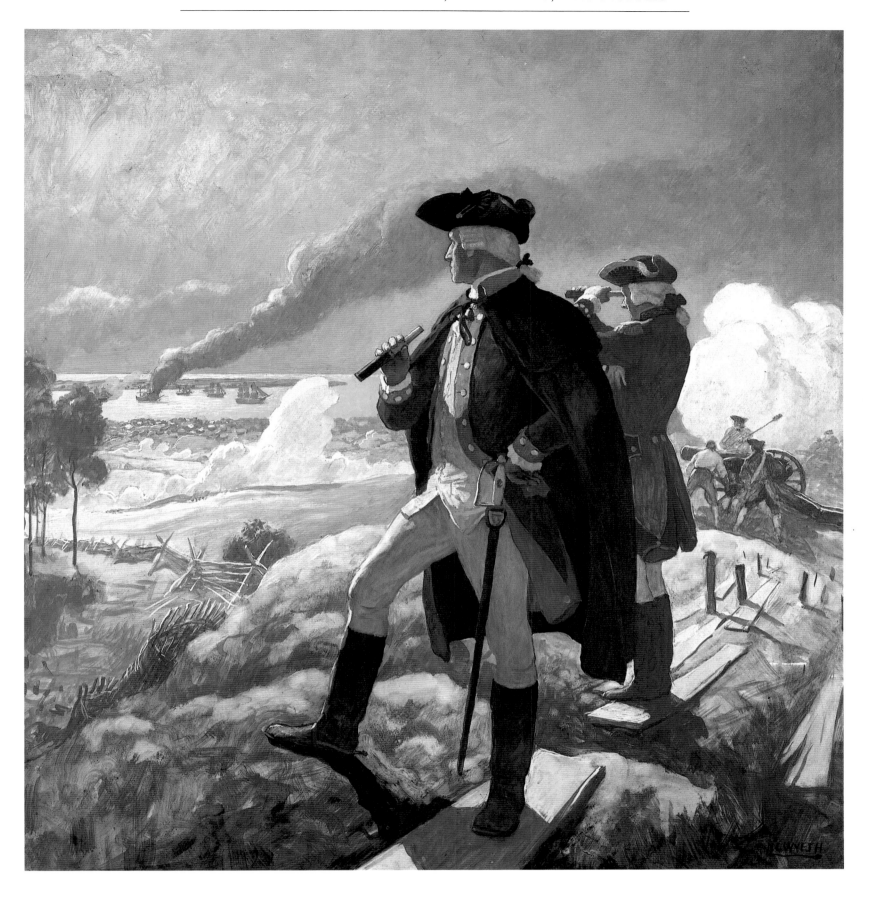

George Washington at Yorktown, 1940
America in the Making, Calendar published for
John Morrell & Company, Ottumwa, IA, 1940
Oil with some areas of tempera on panel, 26¾ × 25 in.
Gift of John Morrell & Company, 1940
From the University Art Collection, Iowa State University, Ames, IA

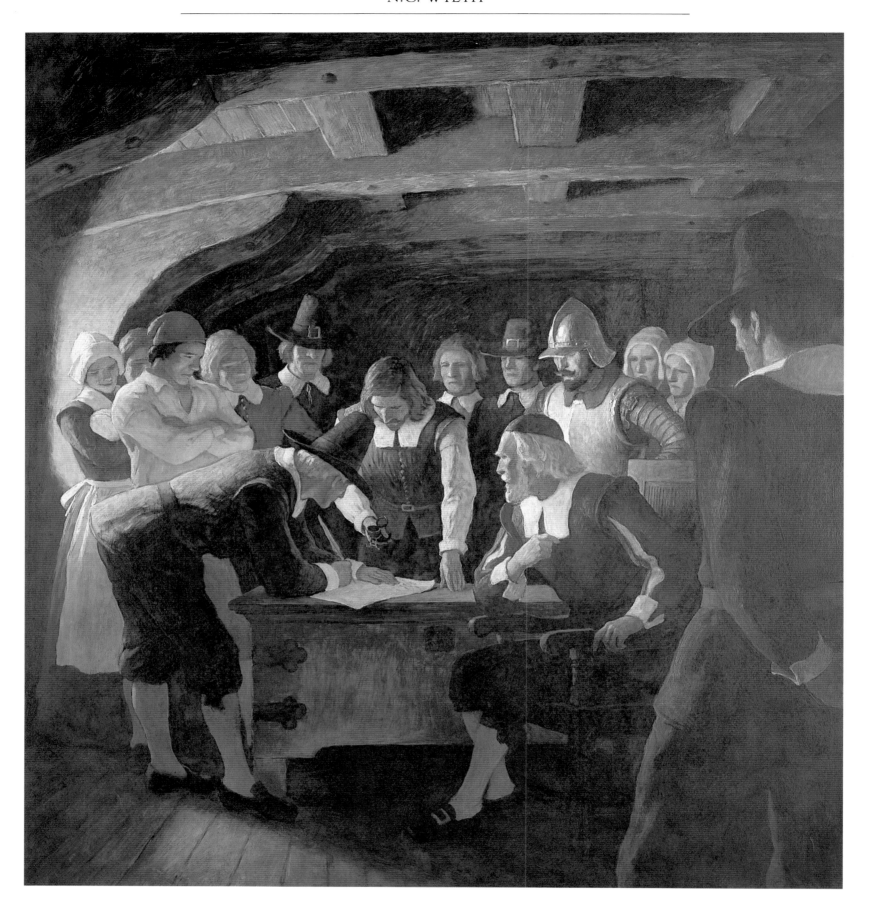

The Mayflower Compact, 1940
America in the Making, Calendar published for
John Morrell & Company, Ottumwa, IA, 1940
Oil with some areas of tempera on panel, 26½ × 24½ in.
Gift of John Morrell & Company, 1940
From the University Art Collection, Iowa State University, Ames, IA

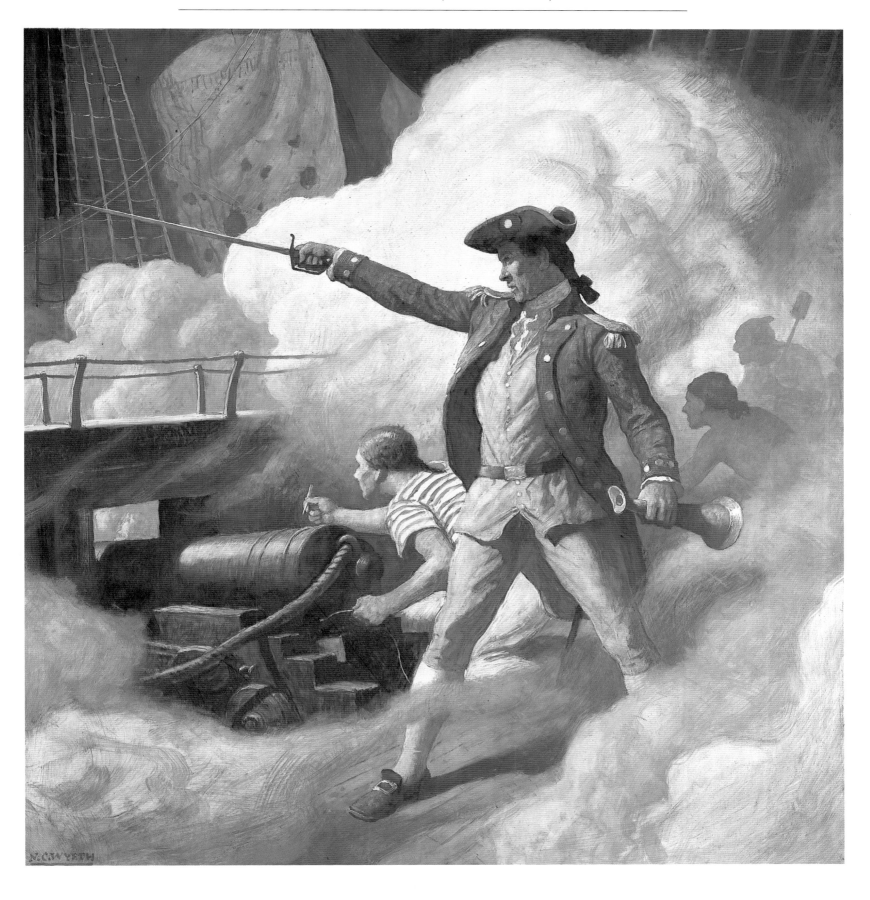

Captain John Paul Jones, 1940
America in the Making, Calendar published for
John Morrell & Company, Ottumwa, IA, 1940
Oil with some areas of tempera on panel, 27 × 25 in.
Gift of John Morrell & Company, 1940
From the University Art Collection, Iowa State University, Ames, IA

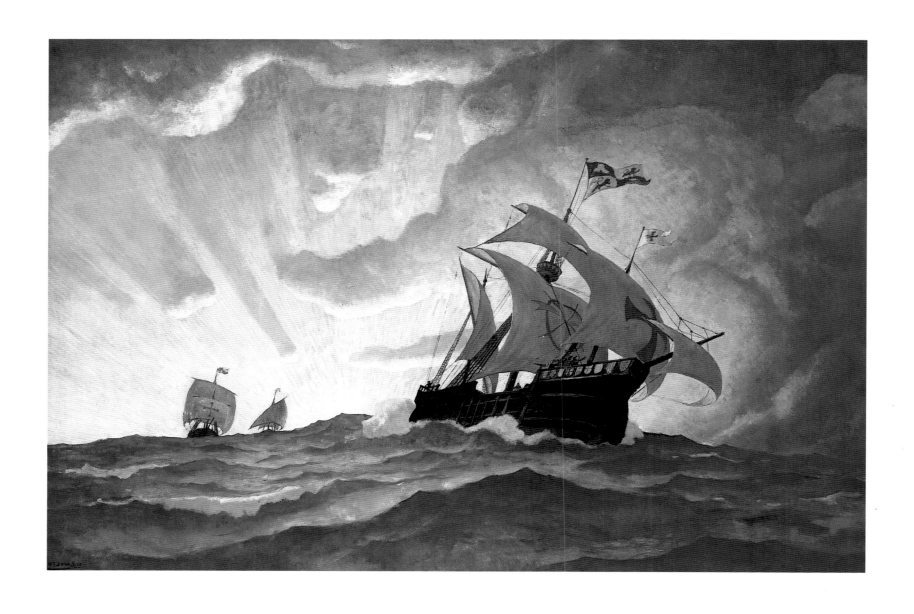

A New World in View, 1943
Our America: Transportation, educational poster
Oil on canvas, 27 × 39½ in.
Courtesy of the Coca-Cola Company Archives, Atlanta, GA

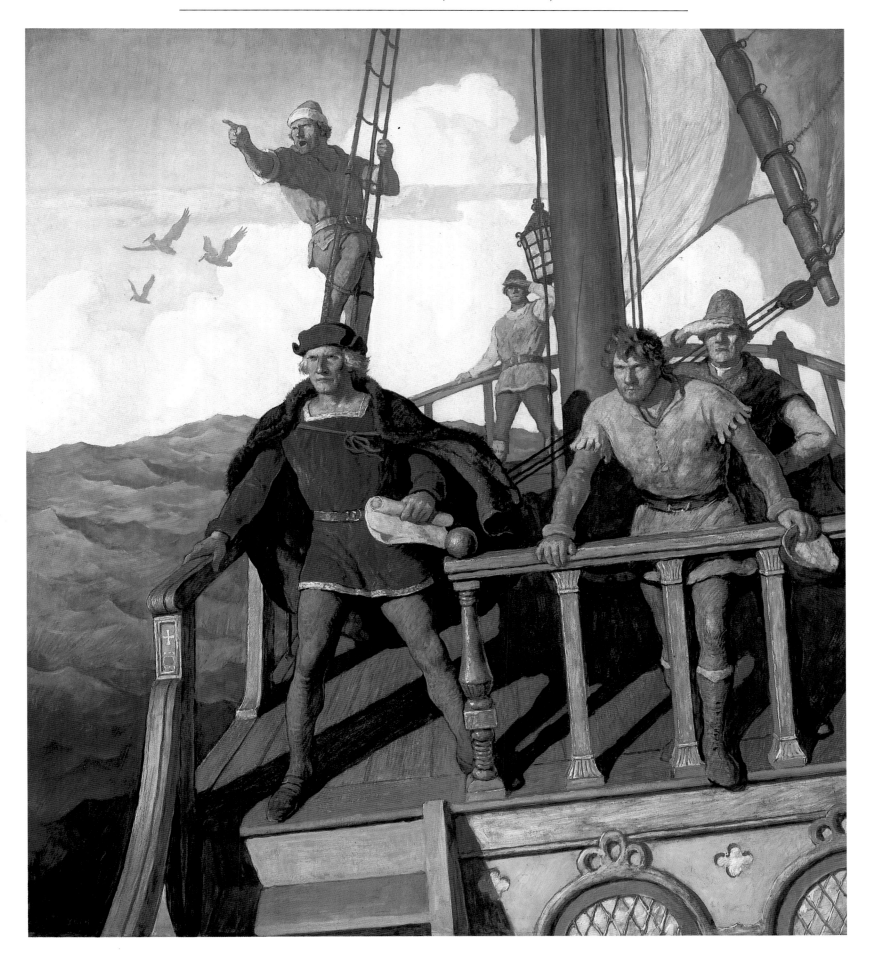

Columbus Sights the New World, 1942
Commission honoring 450th anniversary of
the landing of Columbus
Oil on gesso board, 26 × 23 in.
Photograph courtesy of the Brandywine Fantasy Gallery, Chicago, IL

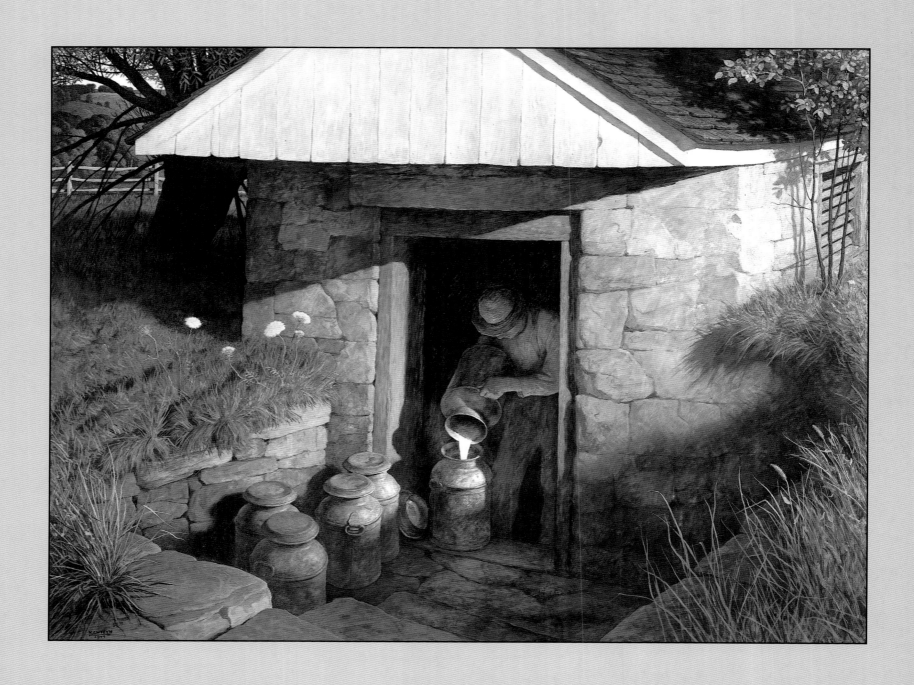

Springhouse, 1944
Tempera on panel, 36 × 48 in.
Special Purchase Fund
Courtesy of the Delaware Art Museum, Wilmington, DE

LANDSCAPES AND STILL LIFES

Newell Convers Wyeth painted landscapes and still lifes throughout his career. Though several of these were of a commercial nature, the subjects he yearned to paint the most were the countryside around him – the fields, the hills, the animals, and the characters he saw and knew there.

Though he found fame and recognition through his commercial illustrations and public murals, and was able to support his family of five comfortably in Chadds Ford with the fees he received for this work, what he enjoyed most were these simpler, freer motifs that were his independent choices for his canvases.

Wyeth portrayed lovely farms in all seasons and various farmhouses and barns located on these acres. Some of these belonged to the artist himself and others were owned by local citizens in his community. He painted more of these artistic satisfactions for his soul in his later years.

He had a show at the MacBeth Gallery in New York in 1937 where Mrs. C.V. Whitney bought one of his paintings for the collection of the Whitney Museum of American Art. Doll and Richards, a Boston gallery that also represented Winslow Homer, gave Wyeth a show at its exhibition space.

In *Nightfall*, Wyeth depicted a spare-limbed farmer standing on a hill with his young daughter, his hand resting on a fence before him. She wears a sweet, gingham dress and looks back to the barn and their homestead and livestock below.

An especially lovely work is *Newborn Calf*, which glows with the charm of rural events and the pleasure of seeing young animals born into the world. A young heifer is posed in front of a white barn, looking contentedly out at the viewer.

The Wyeths bought a house in Port Clyde, Maine, in 1920 and made extensive renovations on their seaside retreat over the next ten years. They called their summer resort domicile "Eight Bells" after a painting by Winslow Homer, one of N.C. Wyeth's favorite artists. Here, too, Wyeth would often paint familiar and favorite scenes, such as *Deep Cove Lobsterman*, a study of a fisherman in his boat out on the tranquil bays surrounding Port Clyde, hauling the catch of the day in his nets. Wyeth and his son Andrew took many walks in Maine and shared a studio space; the second and third generations of the Wyeth family continue painting there today.

Wyeth did not paint many self-portraits but those he did are memorable. One features him in a Christmas stocking cap grinning at the viewer rakishly. A more serious study is a richly painted, investigative exploration of his face and upper torso seated at the easel. His intense gaze signifies his power of perception. This realistic canvas is almost photographic in clarity.

Another tranquil, pastoral setting is described in Wyeth's *The Springhouse*, painted in 1944. Here we see a farmer bending over pouring milk into his buckets after tending to the cows. One of the first farms the N.C. Wyeths lived on was leased out in part to dairymen for their herds and he became familiar with the gestures and patterns of their quotidian routines. Wyeth had also milked cows on his family's farm in Needham, Massachusetts, and could remember the physical movements associated with this chore and paint them as he recalled them. The detail is precise: individual blades of grass can be seen around the springhouse along with tall blossoms of Queen Anne's lace.

Overleaf:
Summer Days, 1909
Oil on canvas, 16 × 20 in.
Collection of Mr. and Mrs. Andrew Wyeth
Photograph courtesy of the Brandywine River Museum

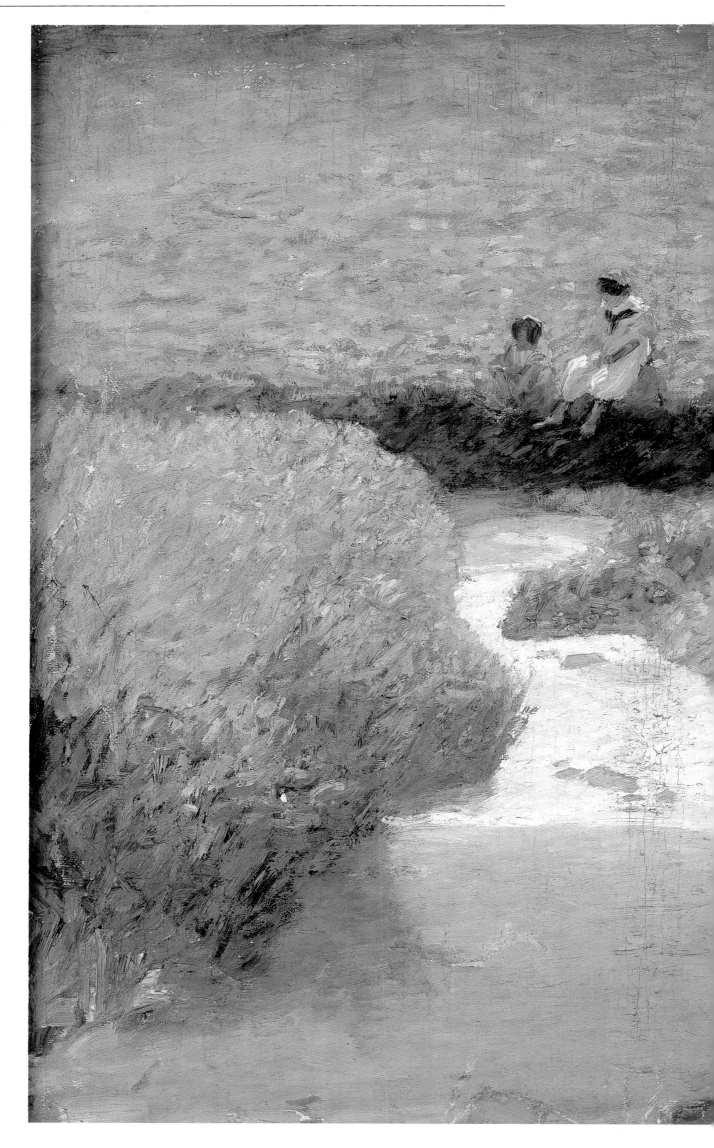

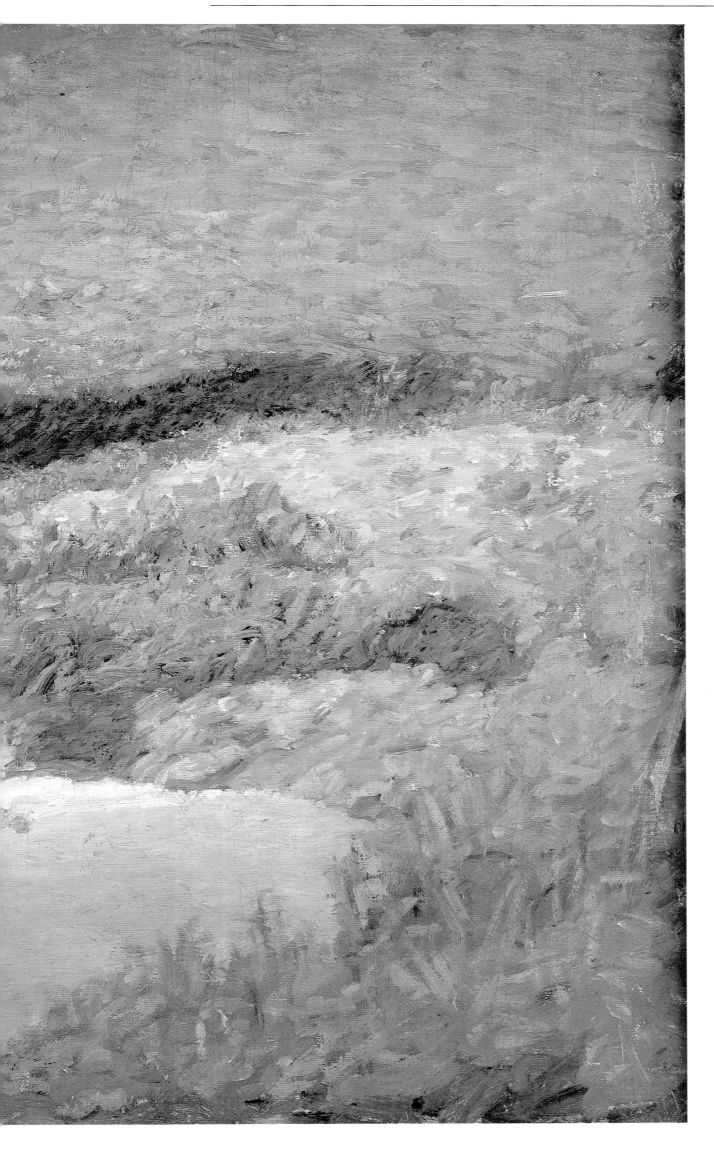

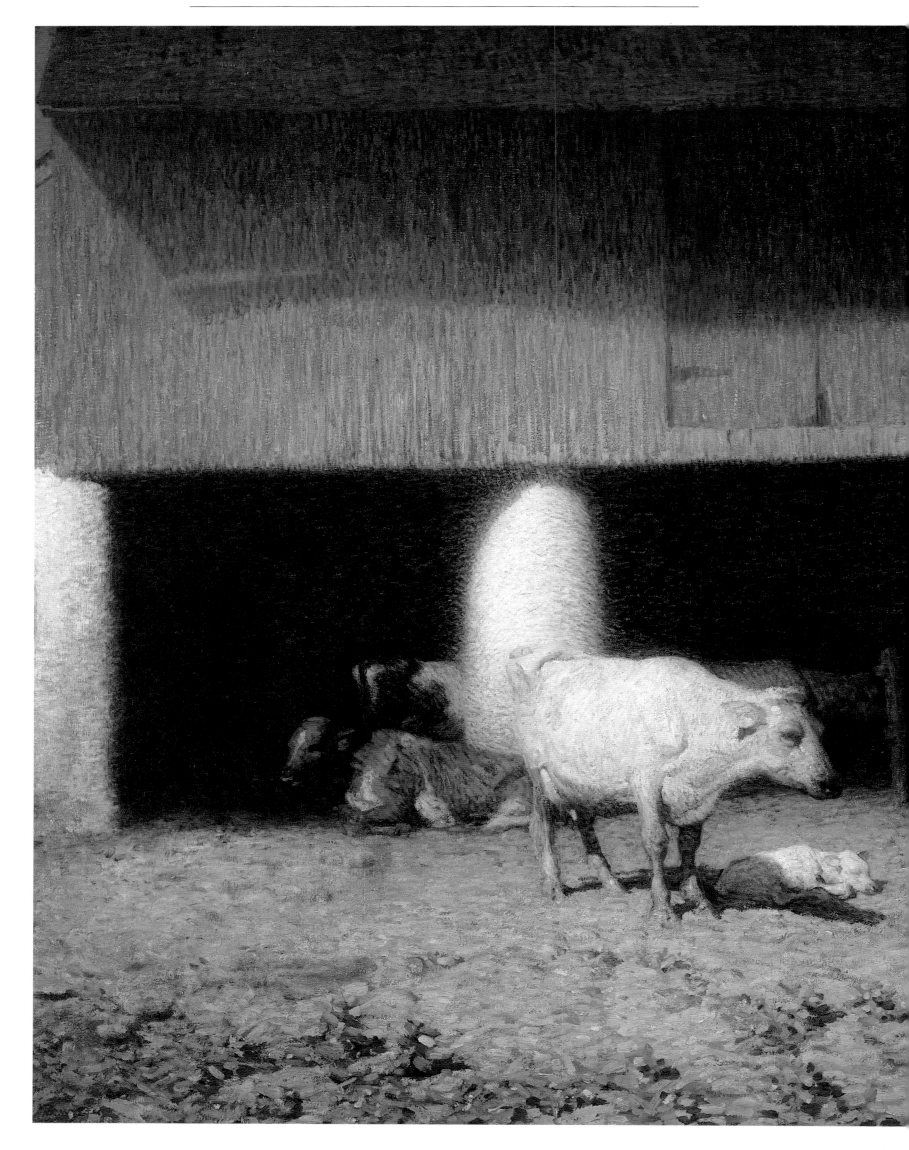

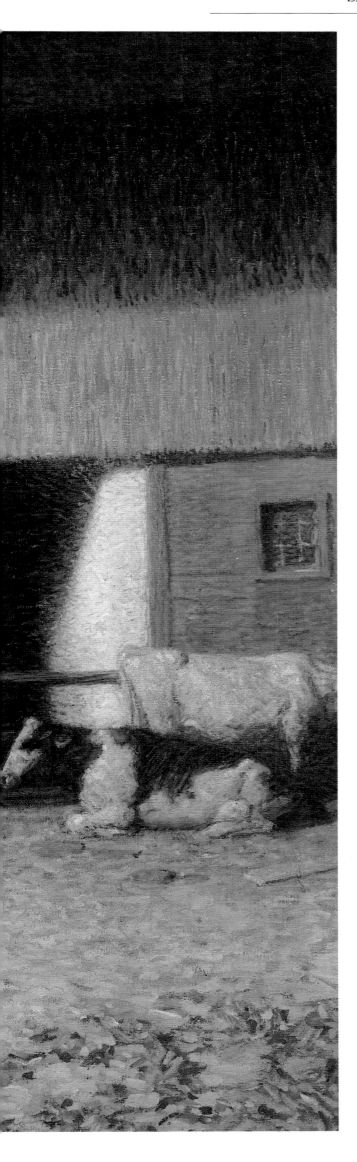

Newborn Calf, 1917
Oil on canvas, 48½ × 53¼ in.
Collection of Mr. and Mrs. Andrew Wyeth
Photograph courtesy of the Brandywine River Museum
Photography by Peter Ralston

Overleaf:
The Fence Builders, 1915
Oil on canvas, 37½ × 49½ in.
Private Collection
Photograph courtesy of the Brandywine River Museum

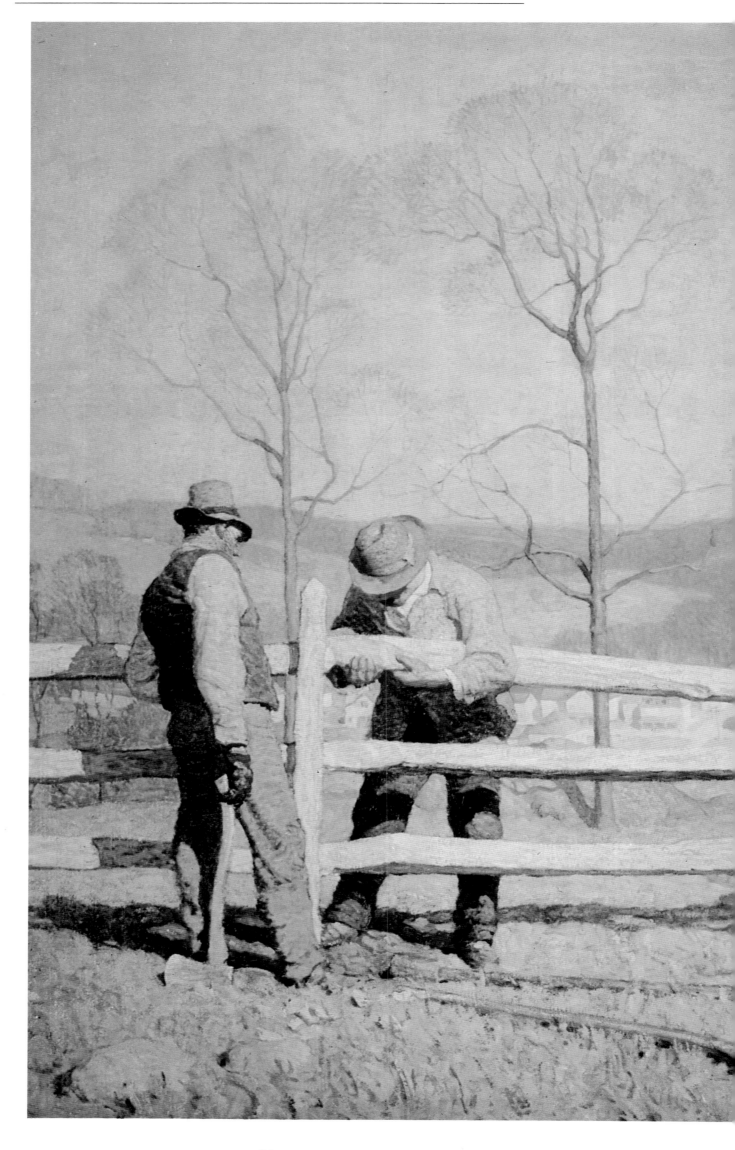

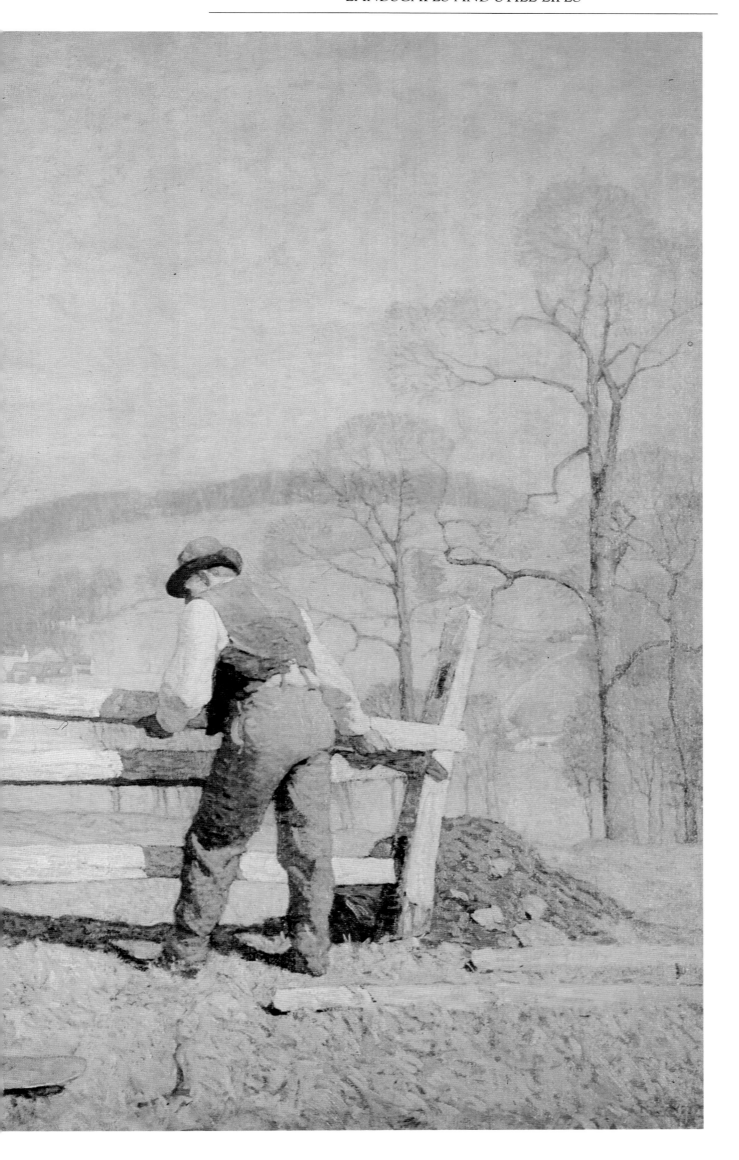

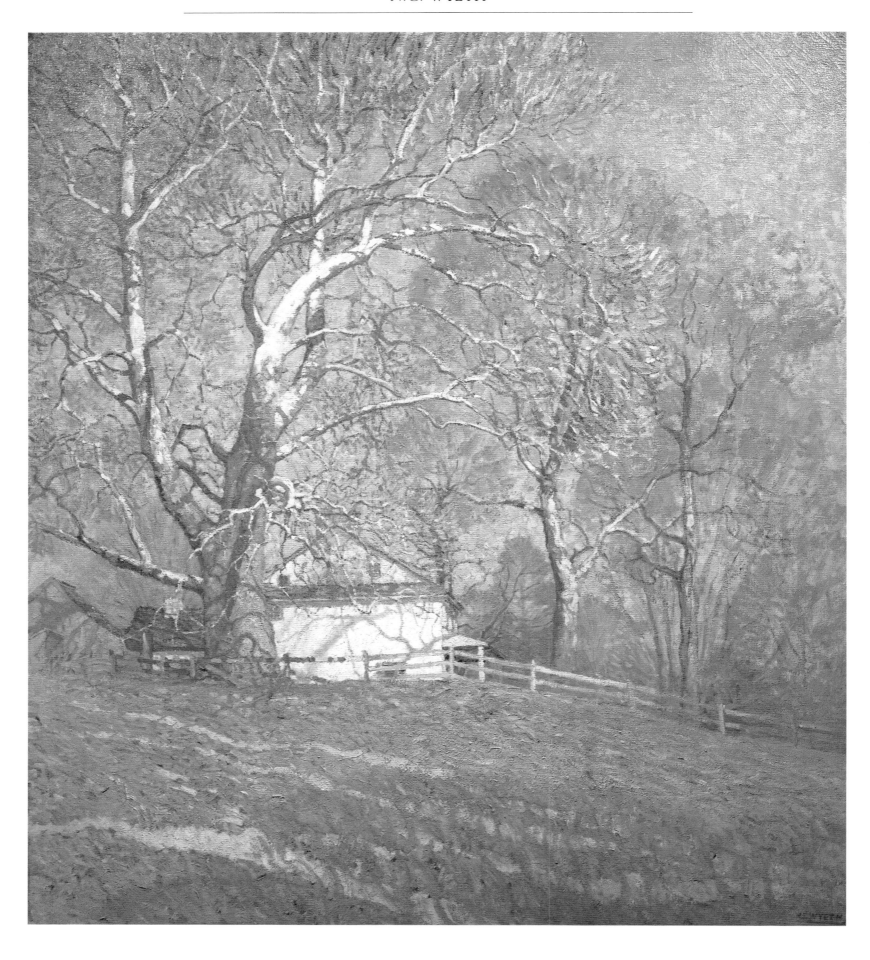

Buttonwood Farm, 1920
Oil on canvas, 48½ × 42¾ in.
Courtesy of the Reading Public Museum and Art Gallery, Reading, PA

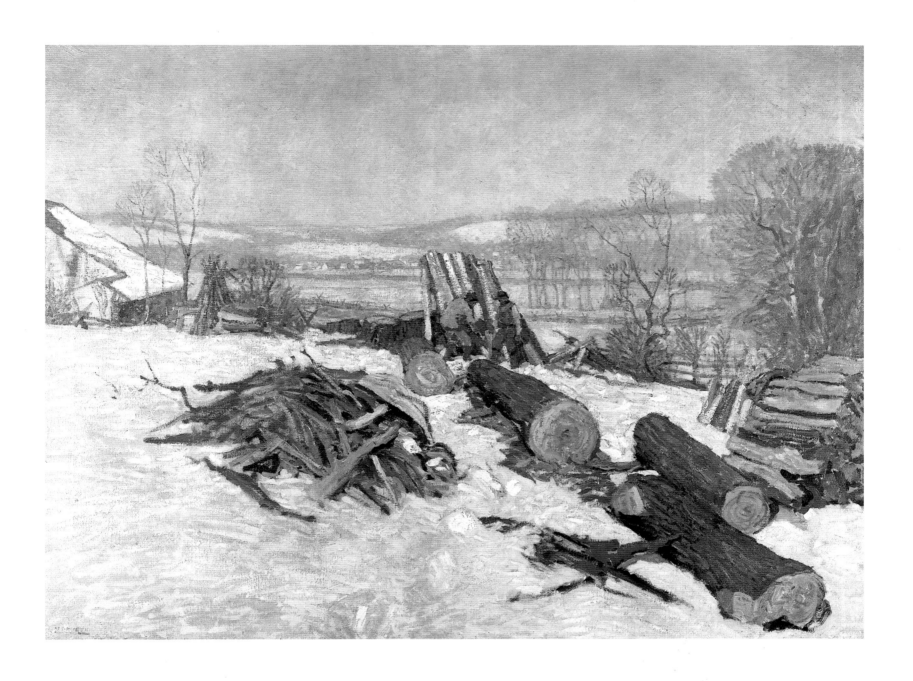

Last of the Chestnuts, 1917
Oil on canvas, 37¼ × 49¼ in.
Collected by C. T. and Claire McLaughlin
Diamond M Foundation Fine Art Collection, Lubbock, TX
Photography by Nicky Olson

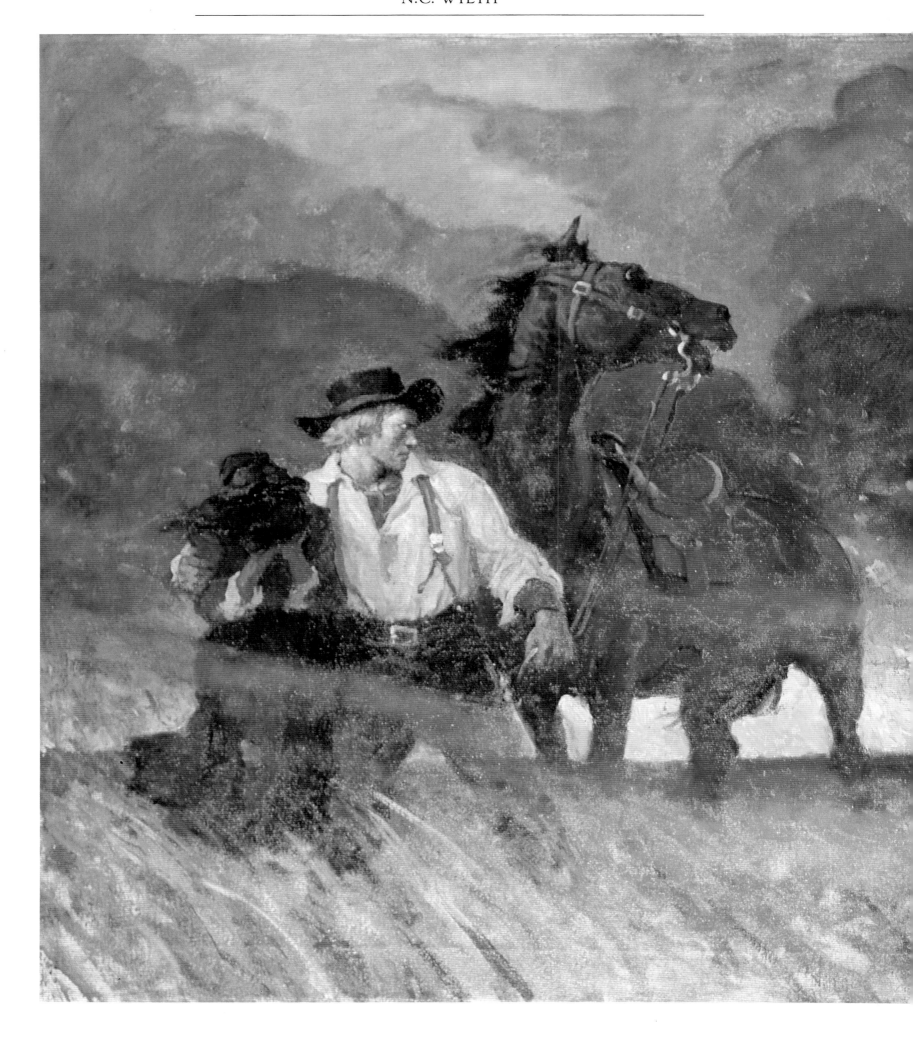

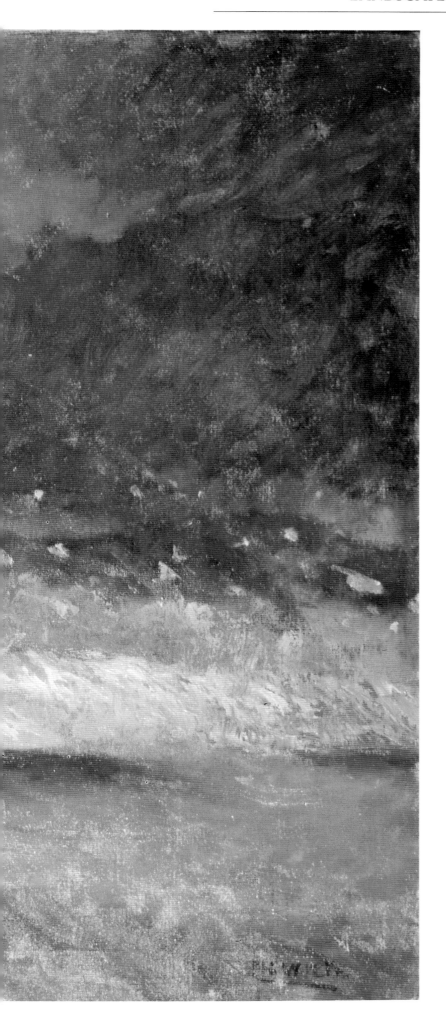

The Prairie Fire, 1922
"Vandemark's Folly" by Herbert Quick
Ladies Home Journal, February 1922
Oil on canvas, 39½ × 41 in.
Collection of Mr. and Mrs. Barton C. Conant
Photograph courtesy of the Brandywine River Museum

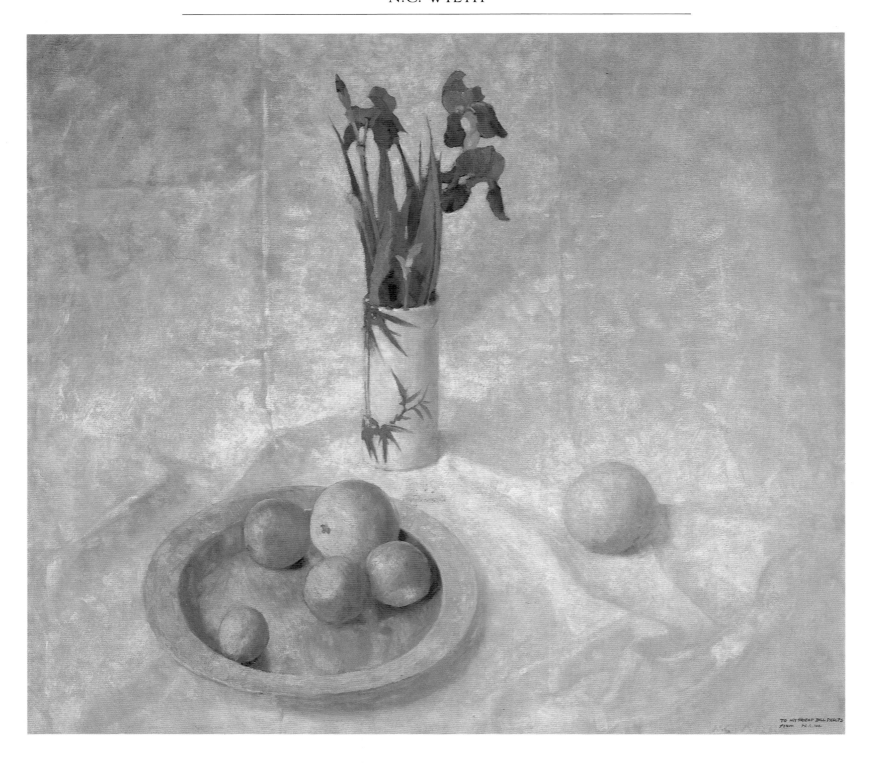

Still Life with Iris and Oranges, c. 1924
Oil on canvas, 36 × 40 in.
Collection of the Delaware Art Museum, Wilmington, DE
Photograph courtesy of the Brandywine River Museum

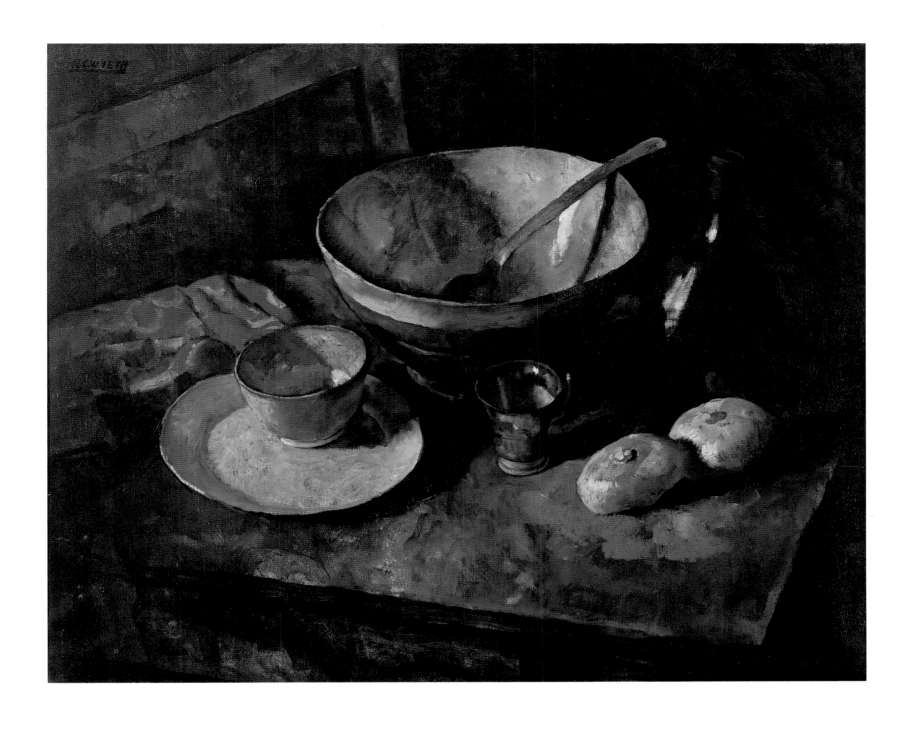

Still Life with Onions, c. 1924
Oil on canvas, 32¼ × 47¼ in.
Given in memory of Clement R. Hoopes by his family and friends
Collection of the Brandywine River Museum, Chadds Ford, PA

Overleaf:
April Rain, 1935
Oil on canvas, 41¾ × 52 in.
Private Collection
Photograph courtesy of the Brandywine River Museum

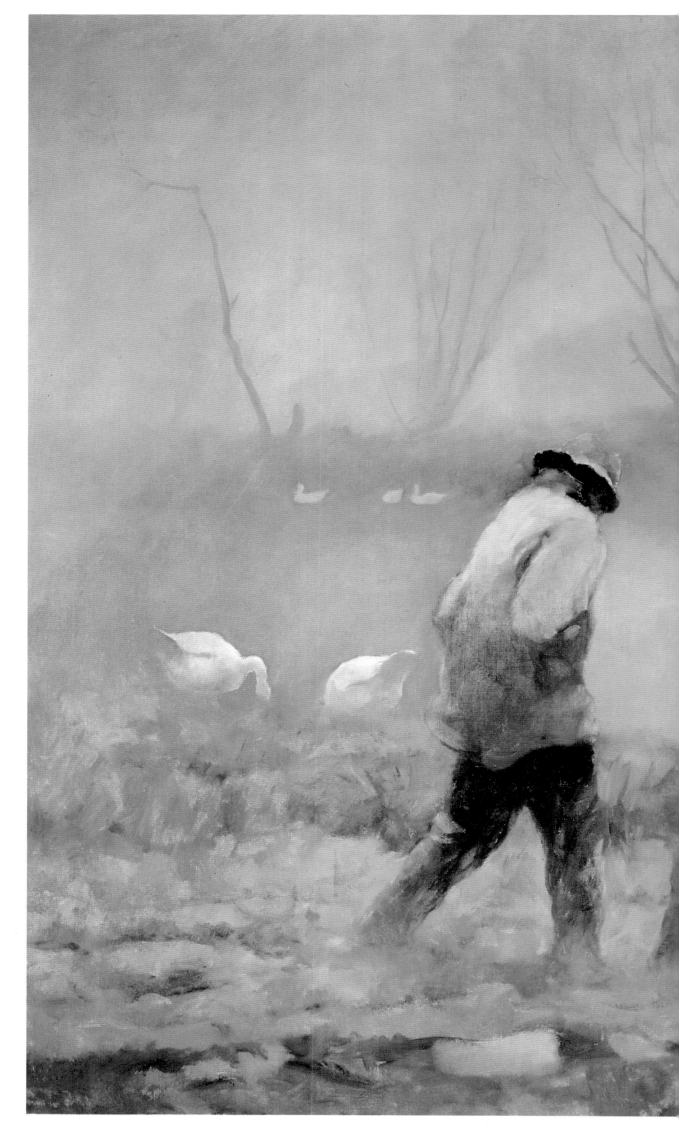

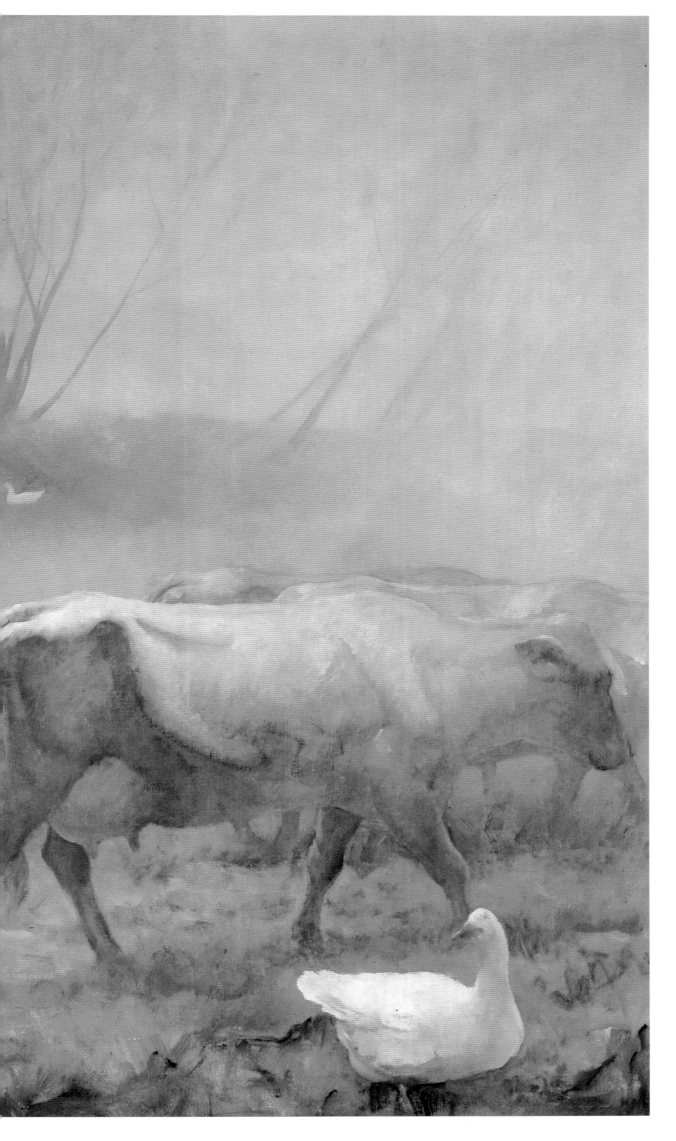

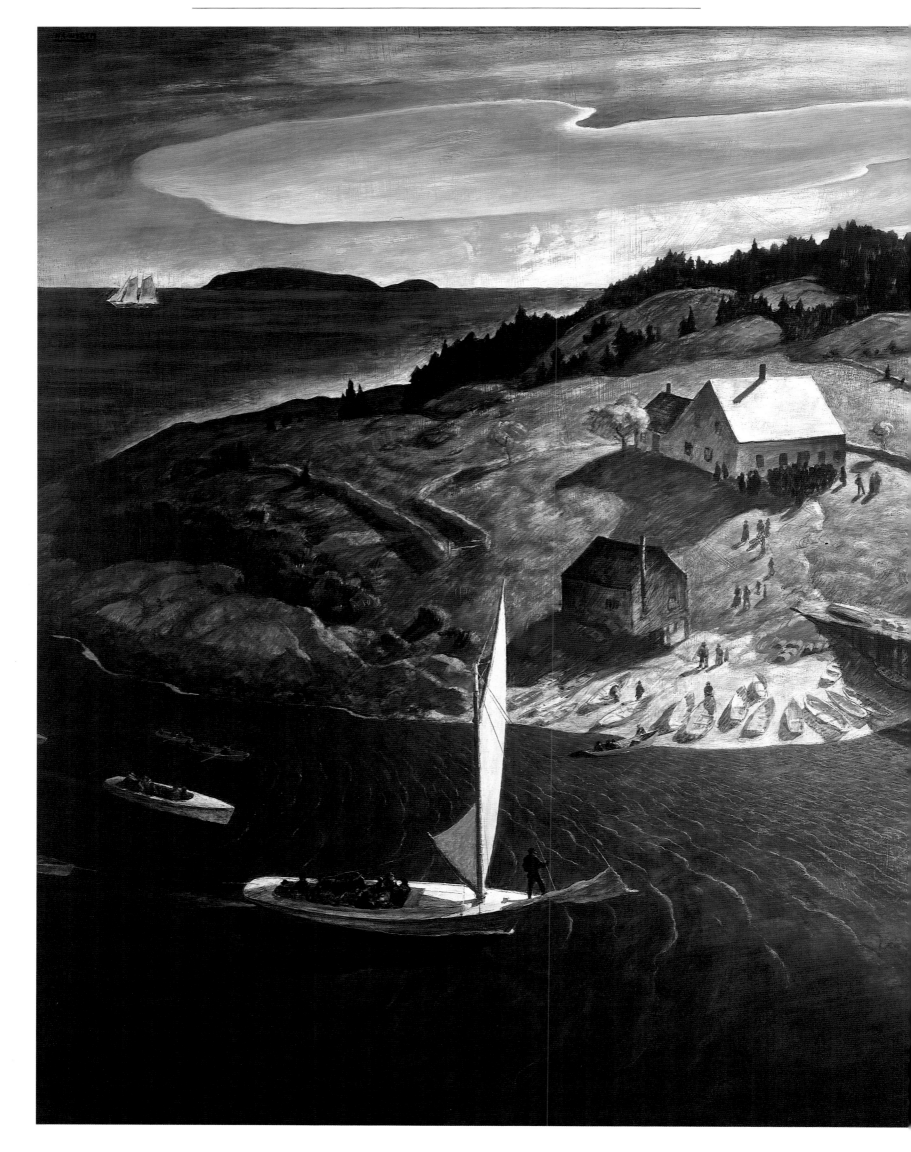

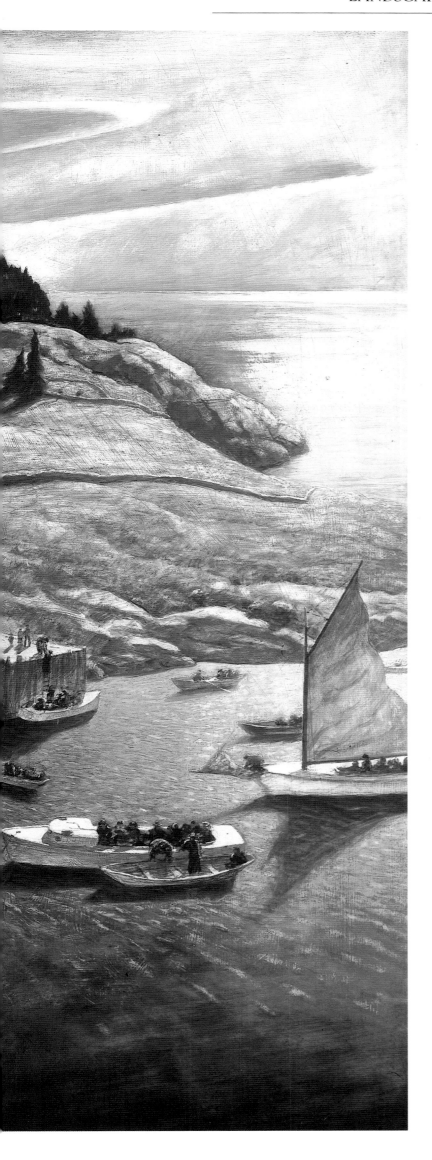

Island Funeral, 1939
Tempera on panel, 47½ × 55¼ in.
The Hotel DuPont Collection of American Art
Photograph courtesy of the Brandywine River Museum

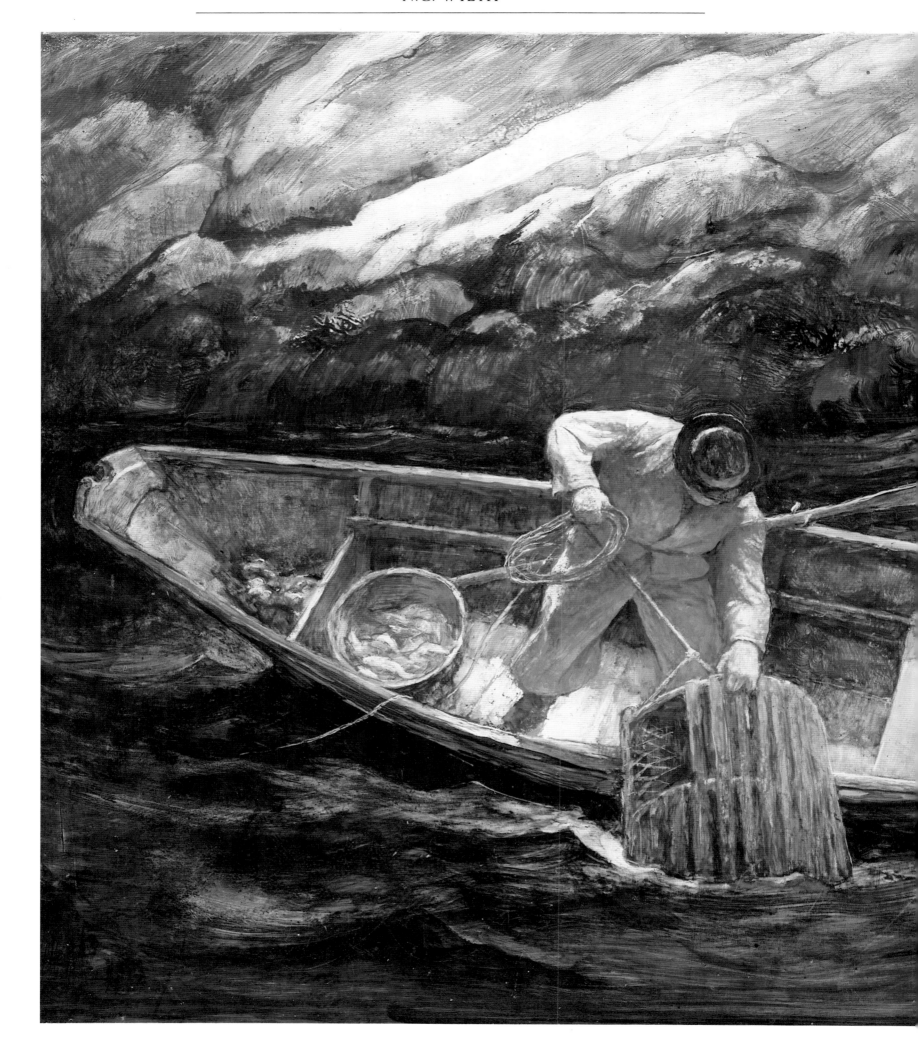

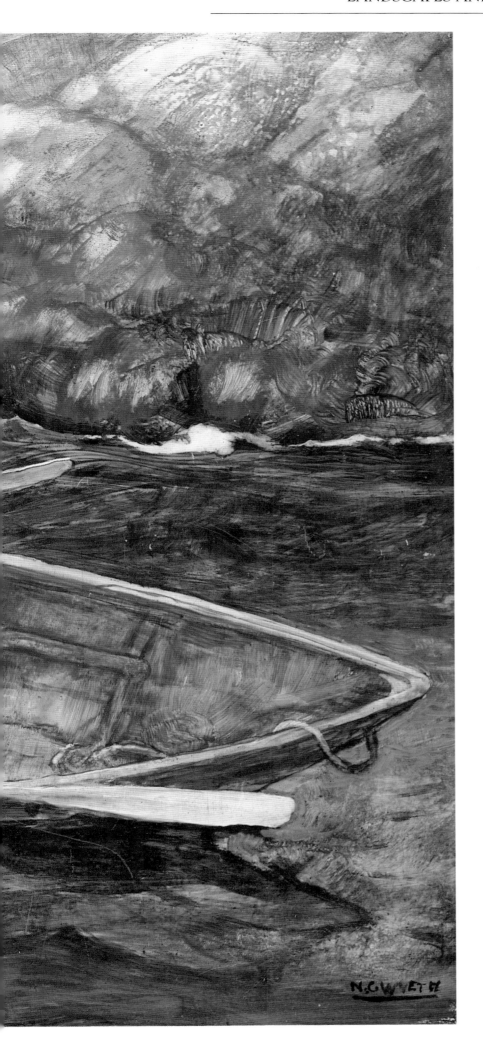

Deep Cove Lobster Man, 1938
Oil on panel, 16¼ × 22¾ in.
Joseph E. Temple Fund
The Pennsylvania Academy of the Fine Arts, Philadelphia, PA

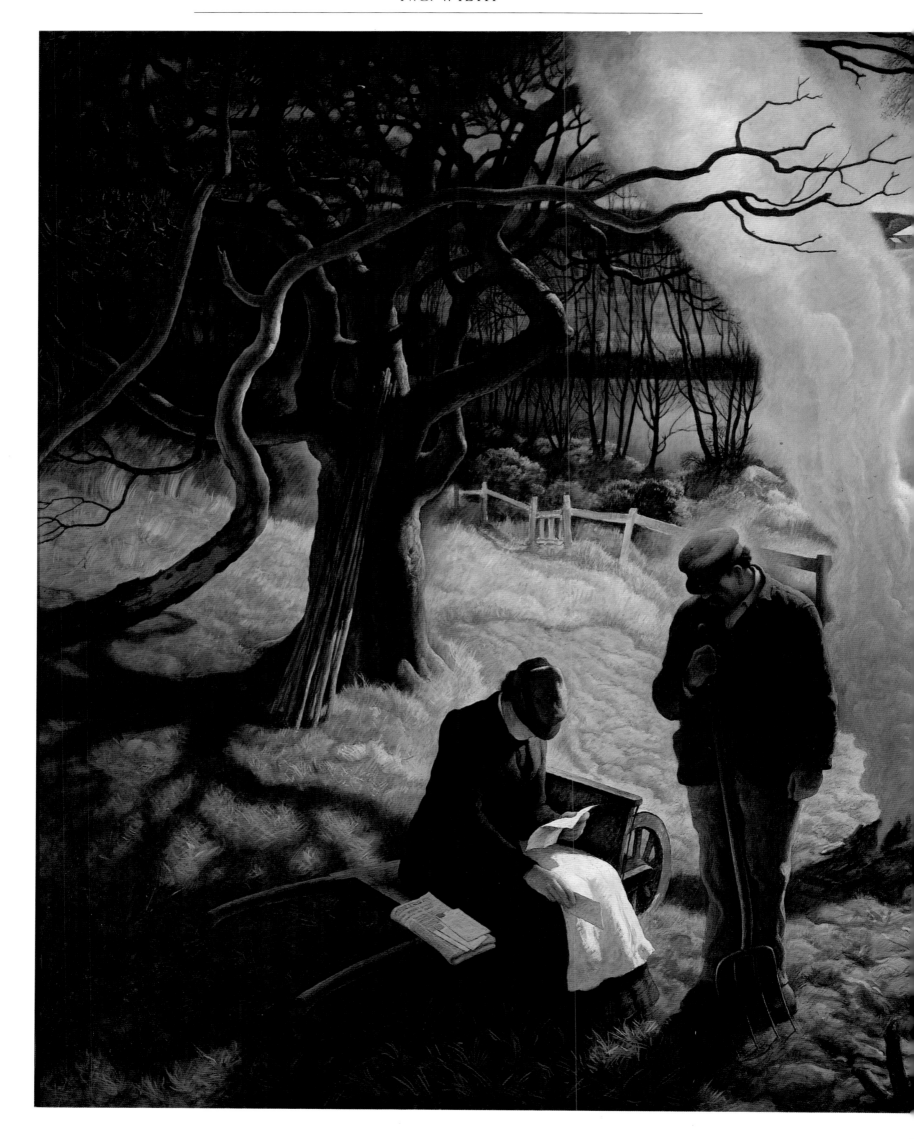

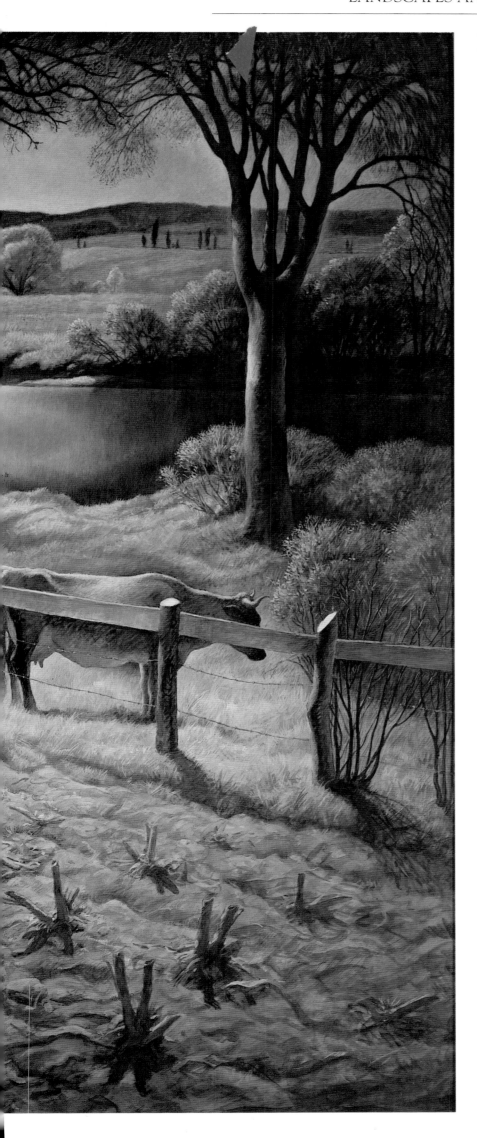

The War Letter, 1941
Tempera on panel, 37 × 46 in.
Given in memory of Deo DuPont Weymouth and Tyler Weymouth
Collection of the Brandywine River Museum, Chadds Ford, PA

Overleaf:
Mrs. Cushman's House, 1942
Tempera, 21½ × 37⅜ in.
Harriett Russell Stanley Fund
Courtesy of the New Britain Museum of American Art,
New Britain, CT

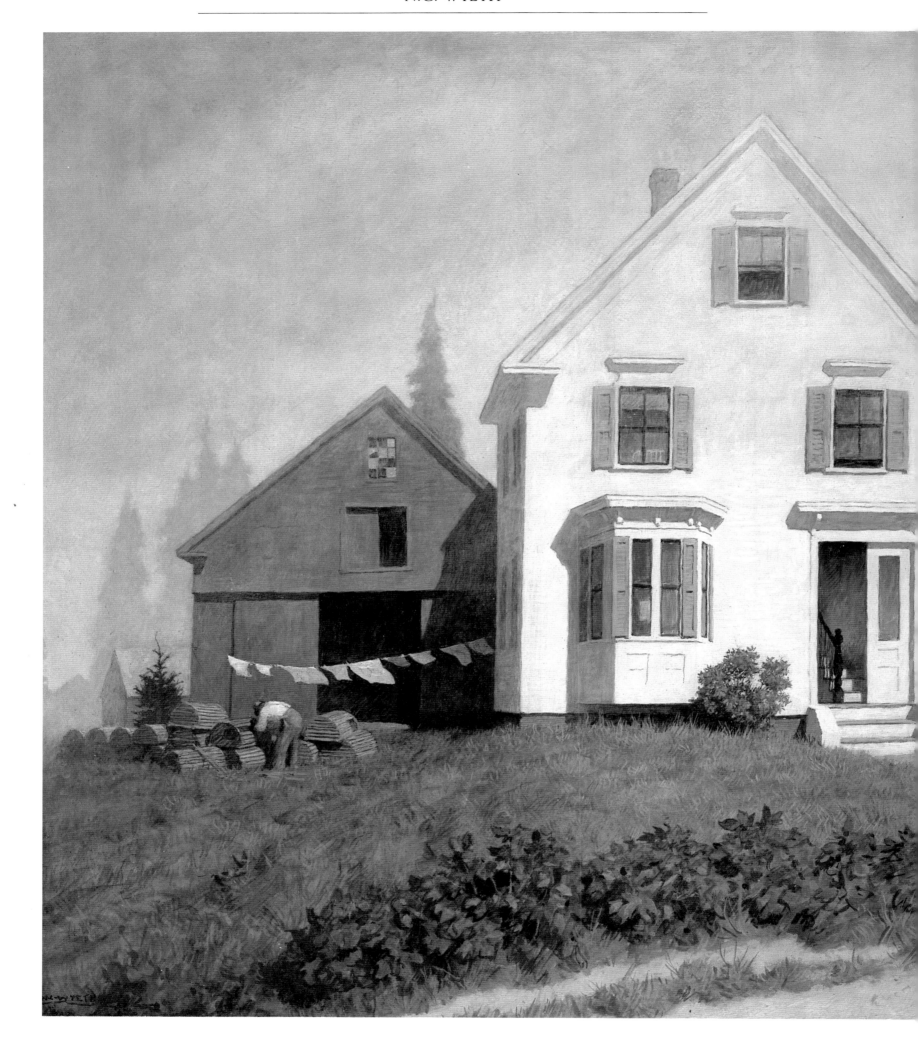

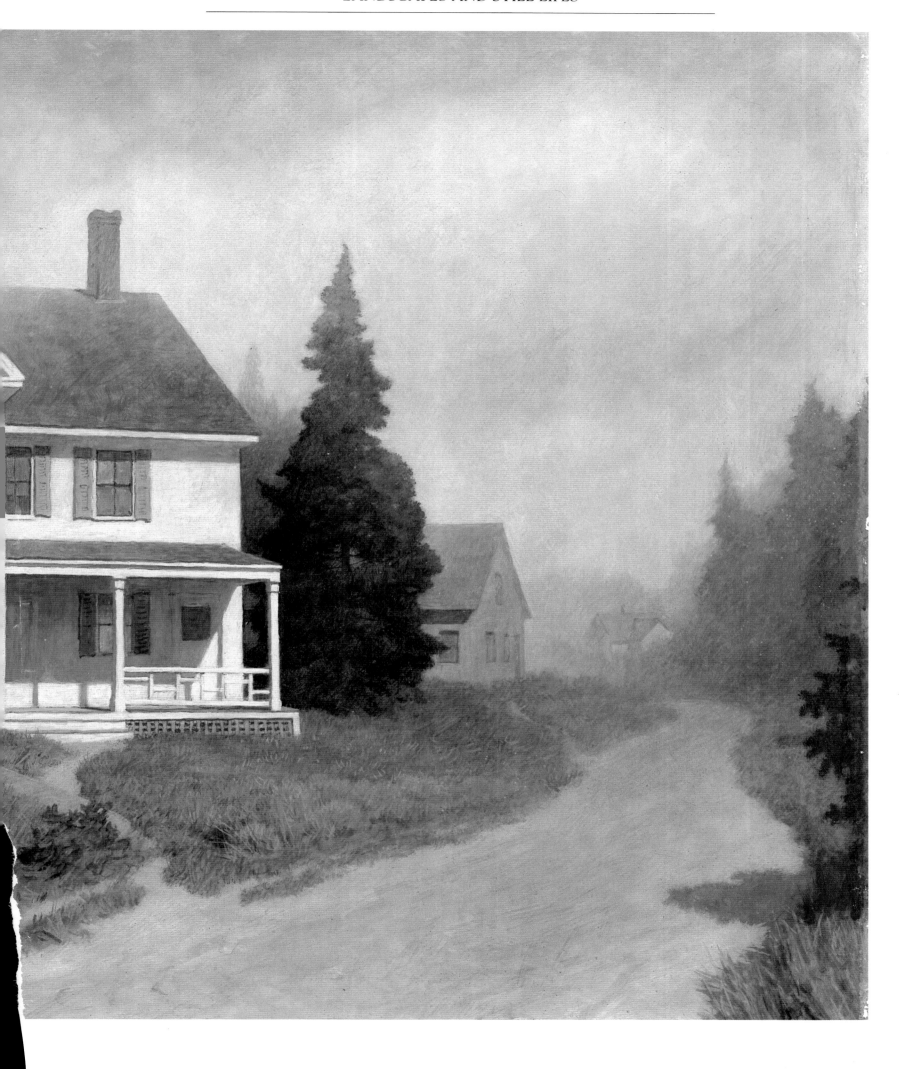

LIST OF COLOR PLATES

Acknowledgments
The author and publisher would like to thank the following people who helped in the preparation of this book: Don Longabucco, the designer; Susan Bernstein, the editor; and Kathy Schneider, the picture researcher.

For their valuable time, assistance and input we would like to thank the staff of the Brandywine River Museum (U.S. Route 1, Chadds Ford, PA). A large collection of paintings by N. C. Wyeth may be seen at this museum.

Photo Credits
Photograph courtesy of the Wyeth Family Archives: 6, 7, 11, 13, 14, 15.
Courtesy of the Delaware Art Museum, Wilmington, DE, Howard Pyle Collection: 8(bottom), 12, 17.

Artworks
Page 8 (bottom): N. C. Wyeth
Sketch of a Man on a Bucking Horse, 1902
Oil on canvas, 26 × 18 in.
Courtesy of the Delaware Art Museum, Wilmington, DE

Page 9 (left): Howard Pyle
The Nationmakers, 1903
Collier's Weekly, June 2, 1906
Oil on canvas, 41¼ × 26 in.
Purchased through a grant from the Mabel Pew Myrin Trust
Collection of the Brandywine River Museum, Chadds Ford, PA

Page 9 (right): N. C. Wyeth

Head of an Indian Woman, 1904
Pencil on paper, 11¼ × 8½ in.
Collection of Mr. and Mrs. Andrew Wyeth
Photograph courtesy of the Brandywine River Museum

Page 10 (left): N. C. Wyeth
The Scythers, 1908
"Back to the Farm" by Martha G. D. Bianchi
Scribner's Magazine, August 1908
Oil on canvas, 37½ × 26¾ in.
Gift of Mr. and Mrs. Samuel L. Kingan
Collection of the University of Arizona Museum of Art, Tucson, AZ

Page 10 (right): N. C. Wyeth
Mrs. N. C. Wyeth in a Rocking Chair, c. 1910
Oil on canvas, 26 × 24 in.
Collection of Mr. And Mrs. Andrew Wyeth
Photograph courtesy of the Brandywine River Museum

Page 16 (top): Andrew Wyeth
Siri, 1970
Tempera on panel, 30 × 30½ in.
© *Andrew Wyeth*
Collection of the Brandywine River Museum, Chadds Ford, PA

Page 16 (bottom): James Wyeth
Portrait of Pig, 1970
Oil on canvas, 48 × 84 in.
Collection of the Brandywine River Museum, Chadds Ford, PA